STOCKPORT MEMORIES

Contents

Introduction

As you turn the pages of 'Stockport Memories' be prepared to enter a world of nostalgia for earlier days in the last century. We make no excuses for such a wallow, as the days when grandma was a lass or that dad lived through are jam packed with memorable events. Older ones amongst us will recall some of them very well, but other times may just link with stories and descriptions that our forefathers wove for us. Taking a stroll down memory lane is something that we all enjoy doing. Some of us have a longer path to travel than others, but we are all fascinated by the recent history of times that are only just out of reach. These are particularly important when linked with the past of our own beloved town. Sadly, when we were young we often took only passing notice of the recollections that an older generation had to share with us, leaving but a sketchy awareness of those former days. Even our own firsthand knowledge can become clouded as we try to recall events, people and places as they used to be. Fortunately, for those who love

to indulge themselves in nostalgia, this book will help jog the memory and bring back to life the days when trams clanked their way along Wellington Road and Morris Cowleys wheeled down Heaton Lane. These were the days long before the words 'pedestrianisation' and 'motorways' were coined. Covering the period from the roaring 20s to the flower power 70s, this collection of stunning photographs, supported by thoughtful and at times provocative text, will help to bring back a flavour of how life was lived in those middle years of the last century. Buildings that are lost to us will reappear as if by magic as the reader turns one page after another. Celebratory days will be relived and even the saddest and grimmest of times will be revisited. Young and old alike can come together to enjoy the flavour of the years that helped mould the modern town as we know it today.

'Stockport Memories' is not intended to be a dry and dusty old history book. It is meant to be a means for the reader to hark back to a century that is not too far behind us, but

is growing more distant with each passing day. The 20th century brought us so much. The aeroplane flew for the first time. Electrical appliances changed the way we ran our households and entertained ourselves. Women were liberated and the country became a multicultural society. Villages grew into towns and industry replaced agriculture as our setting. New and ever wider roads swept away the lanes and cottages of our heritage and little shops became supermarkets. Tower blocks rose on the skyline and the computer chip replaced the brain. Without pictorial records of the past we would only be able to rely on the written or spoken word for our nostalgia. But, with this book, there is a chance to claw back those days of yesteryear. Sit your children down and leaf through the book with them. They are our future, but they must not be allowed to ignore their heritage. Make sure that they have cameras of their own so that they can repeat the process for generations to come. They must learn from our mistakes and build on our successes. Nostalgia does not mean that you are stuck in the past, you are just remembering the good times and shedding a silent tear of when it was less than so. Not everything in our background is wonderful, but it would be a crime to be unable to preserve those bits that were.

Stockport has a rich history and though it is not known if the Romans settled here, it is clear that the ford across the Mersey was a junction place for several Roman roads and some artefacts from the time have been found in the locality that suggest that such an important spot would have had a degree of fortification. What is more certain is that the Saxons settled here in later years. The name 'Stockport' has two possible derivations. It could have developed from the Saxon for a 'stockaded place by a wood'; while other scholars argue that the name really means 'market in the hamlet'. As they say, you pay your money etc if you want the true derivation.

The existence of Stockport was first recorded in the Domesday Book and there had long been a flourishing market in the town before a charter to hold such an event was granted in 1260 during Henry III's reign, following an earlier Charter of Freedom issued in 1220 when the king was still a child and the monarchy very much a regency. A Norman castle dominated the site for many years and was rebuilt and adapted several times before final demolition occurred in 1775. Sir Robert de Stockport, one of the feudal barons so powerful in medieval tomes, played a major role in forming the municipal and administrative nature of the town as he helped establish Stockport as a place that

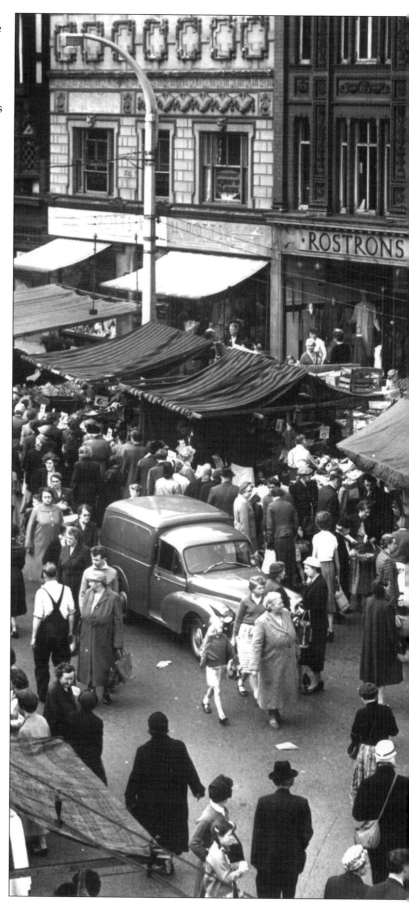

elected its own mayor. This was to form the basis of local government for another six centuries until the 1835 Municipal Corporation Act.

The area relied heavily on agriculture for its economy until the late 16th century when a cottage industry in textiles began to assume importance. There was some rope manufacture and hemp cultivation, but by about 1610 the town was famous for its own 'Stopport' cloth. By the middle of the 18th century, silk was a major industry, as were cotton spinning and hat making. This latter industry, in Victorian times, became an international success, with exports of traditional headgear as well as pith helmets, stetsons and fezzes across the globe. Attention turned to engineering in the 20th century, with such aircraft companies as Fairey and Avro being leading players.

This brief flip through 2,000 years of history now sets the scene for 'Stockport Memories' as we start our look at the last century and rediscover the way we shopped, how we played, the jobs we had and the styles of transport we used to get around. They will all hold something special for each and every one of us delving into the pages of this book. We are going to return to butchers' shops where hares and poultry hung on hooks outside the premises, newsagents who sold 'Film Fun', 'Picture Post' and the saucy 'Reveille' and hair stylists who gave us the bob, the Toni perm and the Purdy. There were bars of Fry's Five Boys, Mackintosh's Munchies, bullseyes and sherbet dips to enjoy, whilst dad lit up a Woodbine or mum a Kensitas with a Swan Vesta. Again we can rub Germolene on chapped legs and drink draughts of Ovaltine, proudly sporting a Robertson's Golly badge on our chests. Men wore suits and ladies went into town wearing a hat, whilst little girls had bobbysox and boys wore short trousers beneath their school blazers. We had conker and marble seasons in the playground, charged around madly in games of tig or 40 a side soccer and groomed our dollies' hair. There were trams to dodge and ticket rolls to collect, conductors to pay and I-Spy books to be filled in on car journeys. A different language of measure was on our lips as we talked of stones and hundredweights, gallons and gills or tanners and half crowns. All this and more will be brought back to life as the reader recalls how it all was when wage packets were tipped up on the kitchen table and internet was what you did with the fish you had just caught.

Town Centre Memories

ramlines running left from Bridge Street into Warren Street along the cobblestones and the dress of the people in the photograph tell us that this is a scene from 1931. Horse drawn trams were popular in the town in the 1880s, but it was electrification of the system that was to provide the impetus for the boom in public transport. The first electric tram ran from Mersey Square to Woodley Station in 1901. With the increase in other road traffic after the first world war, the middle of the road tracks and dependence on overhead cabling meant that the tram's inflexibility was to be its undoing. It was phased out in 1951.

Bridge Street was built as a passage over the river Mersey with a parapet view through Lancashire Bridge to the waters below. Great Underbank is past the bridge, off to the right, and Bridge Street Brow heads away in the distance up the steep slope towards Market Place. This access street was also known as Brierly Brow and Kelso Banke. Thomas Brierly was Mayor of Stockport in 1744. Most of the buildings along here have been demolished, but the Union Bank of Manchester has survived. Money still changes hands here today, but not for banking purposes. It is now an outfitters, though the name 'Bank' has been retained.

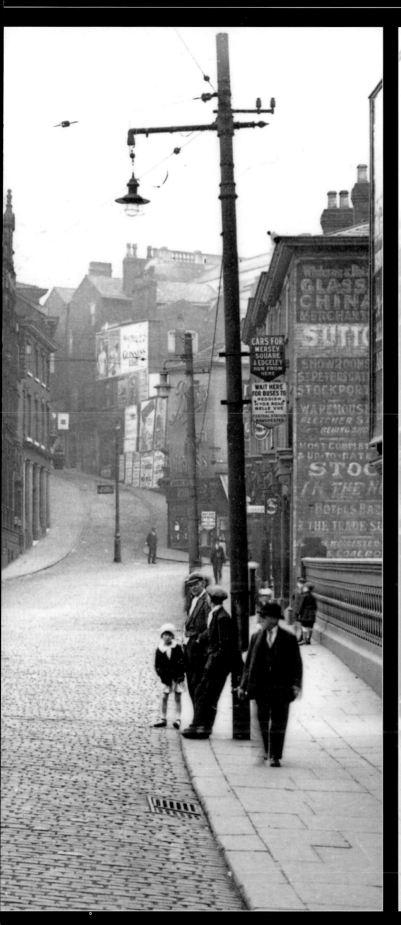

EVENTS OF THE 1930s

MELODY MAKERS

Throughout the 1930s a young American trombonist called Glenn Miller was making his mark in the world of music. By 1939 the Glenn Miller sound was a clear leader in the field; his clean-cut, meticulously executed arrangements of numbers such as 'A String of Pearls' and 'Moonlight Serenade' brought him fame across the world as a big-band leader. During a flight to England from Paris in 1944 Miller's plane disappeared; no wreckage was ever found.

ON THE ROADS

With no driving tests or speed restrictions, 120,000 people were killed on the roads in Britain between the two world wars. In 1934 a Halifax man, Percy Shaw, invented a safety device destined to become familiar the world over: reflecting roadstuds or 'cats eyes'. In dark or foggy conditions the studs that reflected light from the car's headlights kept traffic on the 'straight and narrow' and must over the years have saved many lives.

SCIENCE AND DISCOVERY

By observing the heavens, astronomers had long believed that there in the constellation of Gemini lay a new planet, so far undiscovered. They began to search for the elusive planet, and a special astronomical camera was built for the purpose. The planet Pluto was discovered by amateur astronomer Clyde Tombaugh in 1930, less than a year later.

Above: As traffic on our roads increased, the need for new roads became ever more pressing. Thoroughfares designed for horses and carts in the Victorian era were totally out of sync with modern needs. The men peering through the metalwork on Union Bridge in 1934 were checking on the start of the work on building Merseyway, a major civil engineering project of its era. There is something quaintly British about taking pleasure in watching the progress of others at work. It is hardly top class entertainment, nor is it particularly instructive, but we all do it. However, there was one person who had more than enough on her plate with her offspring. She had no time to stand and stare because three youngsters were proving a handful. Although the dark days of the depression were lifting a little, money was still tight for the working classes. Even those who aspired to lower middle class felt the pinch. We do not know the state of this mum's finances, but like all mothers it is obvious that her children come first. They look to be well wrapped up

against the elements, though the boy is obviously suggesting by his pose that he is tough enough to withstand any inclement weather. The children will be in their 70s today and can comment on how Stockport has changed since that day they crossed the now defunct bridge.

Above: The lady on the left was very grandly attired and strode out in whatever the 1937 parlance for 'strutting her stuff' would have been. She certainly stood out as a member of the middle class with her smart clothing and lofty manner. The woman by her side, dressed somewhat more sedately and, dare we say drably, might just have been a lady's companion. Perhaps her job was to provide a little company for the striking focus of our attention and also to be a form of dogsbody, ministering to madam's whims. They had just crossed Union Bridge, now a structure consigned to the history books. It crossed the Mersey, connecting the two sections of Union Road, and provided access from Great Underbank to Princes Street. When this couple got home they may have discussed the state of the world around them, because change was afoot and trouble was brewing across the continent. Guernica, the cultural capital and spiritual centre of the Basque people, had been destroyed by the bombs of the Condor Squadron of the Luftwaffe, sent by Hitler to help Franco in the Spanish Civil War. The significance of the launching of Britain's latest aircraft carrier, the Ark Royal, would not have been lost on these ladies. Neville Chamberlain became the prime minister that May and embarked on a policy of appeasement that would be a sad epitaph to a political career at the top that ended in 1940.

Below left: When people talk of Merseyway these days they are usually referring to the shopping centre. However, 70 years ago a local would have been talking about the important change to Stockport's centre that saw a major upheaval as an engineering project altered the face of the town for evermore. In Victorian times, the only bridged crossing points in Stockport over the River Mersey were to be found at Lancashire Bridge, from Bridge Street into Tiviot Dale, and at Wellington Bridge where the main road from Manchester to Buxton and beyond could be accessed. In the early 1900s, Mersey Bridge was constructed to link the two sections of Mersey Square that were separated by the river. But, this was not enough for the planners. They embarked on an ambitious scheme to culvert the whole of the river between Lancashire and Wellington Bridges. This work was completed in 1935 and a second phase was begun the following year. This involved extending the culverting from Mersey Bridge to Lancashire Bridge, a distance of some 500 yards, some eight times further than that covered by phase one. This photograph, with British Home Stores to the right, was taken in 1939, with the work well under way. It was completed in 1940 and cars began to drive above a river that had, for all intents and purposes, disappeared from view.

Looking across the 'Bear Pit' balustrade, towards the Mersey public house, now The Chestergate, is a view over Mersey Square that is easily identifiable today. Had the photographer swung the lens to the left, then little of the road that was Merseyway or the shops and buildings around and along it would be recognisable now. Yet, this part is still very similar. The layout of the bollards and bus islands has altered, but even so, the ground level is largely unchanged. Taxis continue to line up along Chestergate, just as they did in this picture. Behind them, across from the site of the original Stockport Grammar School, is one of the town's most interesting tourist attractions that had a major functional use during World War II. The air raid shelters here were specially built to provide protection during the blitz years of the early 1940s. They were one of the few such constructions that were purpose built and could house over 7,000 people as the Luftwaffe did its worst overhead. People even boarded trams from outside of town when the blitz was at its height, confident that they would be safer here than in an Anderson shelter at home. Rock Row, off to the right, is still much the same. The large Ormespers furniture store and other occupants have gone, to be replaced by Outline (figure and fitness) among others, but the main fabric of the building persists, almost in defiance of the development elsewhere across Mersey Square.

Below: In the 1950s, many drivers using Merseyway had forgotten that they were perched above the River Mersey. The prewar scheme that culverted the river was now put to good use as Britain moved towards becoming a nation of car owners. What had once been the preserve of the middle classes became attainable by those from lower social strata as we entered the Harold Macmillan 'never had it so good' years of his premiership. Merseyway was completed at a total cost of about £133,000 and opened to the public on 30 September 1940. Of course, by then, there was little traffic on the roads because of wartime restrictions and it was not until those had been lifted and petrol rationing ended that the new road came into its own. Some of the cars on view when this photograph was taken were considered quite stylish. Notable was the Ford Consul, one of the first to ape America in its particular styling. Alongside it we can spot a Ford Pilot and a light coloured VW Beetle further to the left. This latter car was one of the few continental makes to be seen on our roads at the time and this was also long before the invasion of cars from the Far East. Ironically, Merseyway had a short life as a highway. Within a quarter of a century of its inauguration, the pneumatic drills were hard at work digging it up, converting it into one of the country's first pedestrianised streets and making a start on the creation of the new shopping centre.

Above: In March 1960, cinemagoers to the Plaza, on the far side of Mersey Square, might have opted for the down to earth, gritty style of movie that the British cinema industry was turning out. 'Room at the Top' and 'Saturday Night and Sunday Morning' were warts and all types of films. Alternatively, the section of the public that liked something a little easier on the brain could opt for 'Carry on Nurse', with the gorgeous Shirley Eaton and hilarious Kenneth Williams. There was also 'Tommy the Toreador' with Tommy Steele warbling about that dreadful little, white bull that we all would have loved to see whisked off to the abattoir. Going to the pictures was still part of the courting ritual in those days. A girl expected to be taken to see a film that she could enjoy even while her beau was nuzzling her ear. It was all the better if she could have a bag of Payne's Poppets and a drink on a stick Orange Maid at the interval. That was sheer bliss. Anyway, dad said she had to be back home by 10.30 and that meant time for just a quick kiss before saying goodnight and letting her chap down lightly. The Plaza is one of the few buildings in the area to have survived the redevelopment phase. Built in 1932, it opened with a seating capacity of 1,850.

Below: The view across Mersey Square in c1960 is completely different from the present vista. Then, we had the fire station and bus garage to look at, but these went later in the decade to make way for the Merseyway Shopping Centre. One nice, little period piece from the time can be spotted to the right. The motorcycle and sidecar has almost completely disappeared from our roads today, but it was once far from a rarity, though never a common sight. The combination was a fairly economical way of getting about, but not the safest mode of transport ever invented. A small family could be accommodated with dad at the handlebars, mum behind and junior in the sidecar. The one in charge of the bike might or might not have bothered with a crash helmet, but his passengers probably made do with a headscarf for one and school cap for the other. As speeds and the volume of traffic increased, so did the number of fatalities. It was also not very good for the 60s' version of street cred to turn up to take a girl out for the evening on board a motorbike combination. This style of vehicle was very popular with the roadside assistance services, such as the AA and RAC. Riders could carry basic repair kits and spare parts in their sidecars as they responded to some emergency phoned in to HQ from one of the roadside telephone boxes that could be accessed by a key given to every member. Subscribers to the AA or RAC were given badges to affix to their radiators and were greeted by a salute from a mobile engineer whenever he passed by.

Above: Merseyway is now one of the walkways into the shopping centre, but in the late 50s and early 60s it was a busy road into Mersey Square. Little of what can be seen here now remains, though the Mersey Hotel that sold Wilson's beers is still on the corner under the name of The Chestergate. The Morris Traveller, waiting to turn right, is something of an icon from this era. Powered by a Morris Minor 1000 engine, it had all the attributes of the popular saloon, designed by Alec Issigonis. In addition, its shooting brake appearance and wooden slats along the bodywork lent it a jolly, rural feel, setting it apart from the more down to earth urban cars. Although it is some 35 years since the last models were manufactured, Travellers and Minors are still prized by their owners and receive lavish and loving care. Periodically, rallies are held and proud

owners show off second hand models they have cleverly restored. On the day of this photograph, there must have been a heavy increase in traffic anticipated. Two policemen, with their white gloves and arm pieces, were preparing to take up station on traffic duties. The drivers who were getting used to this part of town becoming a serious bottleneck welcomed their assistance. Merseyway tended to funnel cars to this junction where everything ground to a halt during rush hour.

Left: By 1967, the redevelopment around Mersey Square that was to produce the shopping centre and other emblems of so-called progress was well under way. The reader might not have thought so from this photograph, because the completion date was some three years away. The work was started several years before and many Stockport residents became used to seeing the mixture of metalwork, concrete and mud all around the area and wondered, with a resigned sigh, if there was ever to be light at the end of the tunnel. Six long years was a fair chunk of time to have to put up with such disruption. Shoppers heading into town in the 21st century now regard the shopping precinct as Stockport's hub, but before the redevelopment in the late 1960s, Mersey Square was much more the focal part of town. Traffic was funnelled into it via Merseyway and both sections of Wellington Road.

Today, Mersey Square seems much more compact than it once was as the redeveloped areas seem to have squashed it as they loom with an air of self importance that says, 'We are the controlling force, now'. But, their day will come. At some stage in the future some bright spark will decree that public taste has altered and town centre shopping malls will disappear. Individual stores thought that they were immortal and were proved wrong. Something will come to do the same to precincts.

Above: On a gloomy November day in 1967, the creation of the Merseyway Shopping Centre was about half completed. The finishing touches would not be added until 1970, bringing to a conclusion the mammoth six year project. The massive network of girders, concrete, reinforcing poles and giant cranes somehow came together to produce the epitome of the modern shopping experience. Like it or not, it was what customers wanted at the time. It is only now that many of us try to hark back to the days of the individual shopkeeper, typically when it is too late. This has led to our children being almost totally ignorant of true nature of some of the food that we eat. French beans do not grow all the same size with their ends chopped off and sited in a tray wrapped in film. Nor is a carrot quite as orange looking in its natural state as it appears on the shelf. Ask any youngster where bananas come from and he will reply 'Asda'. How can anyone expect decent service and advice at a supermarket butcher's counter? There a customer is faced by a youth who does not know his rump steak from his elbow and was selling socks in the clothing section five minutes earlier. But, we shoppers asked for it in the 1960s and, boy, did we get it from the 1970s onwards. Want to be measured for a new suit? Forget it.

EVENTS OF THE 1960s

HOT OFF THE PRESS

Barbed wire, concrete blocks and a wide no-man's-land divided East from West when a reinforced wall was built right across the city of Berlin in 1961. Many East Germans escaped to the West at the eleventh hour, taking with them only the possessions they could carry. The Berlin Wall divided the city - and hundreds of family members and friends - for 28 years until the collapse of Communist rule across Eastern Europe. Who can ever forget those scenes in 1989, when ordinary people themselves began to physically tear down the hated wall?

THE WORLD AT LARGE

'One giant leap for mankind' was taken on 20th July 1969, when Neil Armstrong made history as the first man to set foot on the moon. During the mission he and fellow-astronaut 'Buzz' Aldrin collected rock and soil samples, conducted scientific experiments - and had a lot of fun jumping around in the one-sixth gravity. Twenty-one hours and thirty-seven minutes after their landing they took off again in their lunar module 'Eagle' to rejoin Apollo II which was orbiting above them, proudly leaving the American flag on the Moon's surface.

ROYAL WATCH

Princess Margaret's announcement in 1960 that she was to wed photographer Antony Armstrong-Jones (later Lord Snowdon) brought sighs of relief from her immediate family. Just five years earlier the people of Britain had sympathised as the princess bowed to public and private pressure, ending her relationship with Peter Townsend, Prince Philip's former equerry. The Church (and the Queen, as its Head) frowned on the liaison as Townsend was divorced. Her marriage to Lord Snowdon itself ended in 1978.

Mersey Square, seen at the start of the 1960s, illustrates how dependent we still were on public transport in those days, even with the boom in private motoring. Hopping on a bus to do our shopping in town was part and parcel of our way of life. There were few supermarkets and such things as out of town retail parks, where a car is essential for access, were for future generations. As children we enjoyed bus travel as a necessary facet of normal life. Many modern youngsters view it as a thrill, so commonplace has the car become. Today's grandparents will tell their little ones about the way in which you got on board the bus and a conductor or the female version, often called a 'clippie', walked up and down the aisle selling tickets after you were seated. Every so often an inspector jumped on board to check that the conductor was doing his job properly and to make sure that no passenger had overridden his paid destination. This scenario provided the backdrop for the long running TV sitcom 'On the buses', with Reg Varney and Stephen Lewis doing battle as the driver and conductor who

constantly at loggerheads. As we look across the square in this panorama from 45 years ago, the fire station, bus garage and a row of shops on the corner of Princes Street were doomed to disappear when the Merseyway Shopping Centre was built. The church spire in the distance belongs to St Thomas', Heaton Chapel.

Below: By 1960, Mersey Square was a very busy part of town. Car ownership had rocketed and many families found that they could now afford to run their own saloons. This changed working patterns as workers became more mobile and were able to live at greater distances from their places of employment. It also added a greater strain on our roads as the growing volume of traffic meant that wear and tear increased on highways that had never been built to withstand such use. Modern car drivers know the problems of rush hour traffic, but it is not a new phenomenon. Perhaps we now have twice the number of vehicles on the move, but the roads of 45 years ago were half the width. Older two lane roads were clogged just as badly as modern four lane bypasses and ring roads. Looking across to the George public house on the corner of Wellington Road North and Heaton Lane, a bus is just coming into view. The advert on the side is for Player's cigarettes. In 1960, cigarette advertising was everywhere. Some of it was less than subtle. Pictures of handsome men and good looking women, fags dangling from their fingers, hinted that puffing on the appropriate brand made you more attractive. Some even hinted at a therapeutic effect, such as the menthol flavoured Consulate that was 'as cool as a mountain stream'.

Top right: The photographer was stationed close to the Bridge Street and Princes Street junction in 1962 to take this picture looking north along Tiviot Dale. This was once one of the main routes into the town centre for traffic coming from the direction of Lancashire Hill and the environs of Oldham and Ashton. Today, this view in between the King's Head and Tiviot Hotel is out towards

Great Egerton Street and the M60 motorway and the once busy road is now something of a backwater. During the year that this photograph represents, Britain experienced a number of political and social shifts. James Hanratty was hanged for murdering Michael Gregsten in a layby on the A6, but there was still some unease about the quality of the evidence that convicted him and this helped the subsequent Labour government abolish the death penalty in late 1964. The first real word of warning for years to the Tory party that its tenure at 10 Downing Street was in jeopardy came when the Liberals won a sensational by-election victory at Orpington. The old order was in trouble as modernists came to prominence. One of the last bastions of the amateur in British sport crumbled as the last cricket match between the Gentlemen and the Players took place at Lord's. In January, Decca turned down a request for a recording contract from a young group of musicians called the Beatles. Parlophone took a chance and in October 'Love me do' was released. Decca moguls reached for revolvers and aimed for their feet.

Right: Merseyway is laid out today in very similar fashion to this look in the summer of 1968. Marks and Spencer and FW Woolworth, stores that also front Princes Street, continue to dominate this part of town. The staircase

towards the top of the picture has been remodelled to give it a more spiralled effect and there is now a kiddies'

roundabout beyond it. Large boxes with flowers and trees inside have replaced the square lawns and the paving stone deign is a little different, but it is still basically much as it used to be as pedestrianised shopping came to be part and parcel of our way of life. Looking along Merseyway from the Bridge Restaurant towards the British Home Store, a trio of young women take the eye. They were obviously dedicated followers of fashion, as the Kinks used to say, and looked to Mary Quant for ideas for their wardrobe. This young designer set the trend from her Chelsea boutique in the mid 1960s and girls took to her styles and cuts in a way that revolutionised female fashion almost overnight. Away went the look that was akin to an up to date version of clothing their mothers might wear and in came a wholly different approach that said, 'I am who I am'. Mini dresses with hemlines like pelmets were must have items. The older generation was shocked and preachers in pulpits banged on about the decadence of youth.

The early 20th century prosperity of many northern towns was based on the industrial investment of the previous century. Even in the mid 1970s, as seen from this aerial view of Portwood and the town centre, remnants of the industrial revolution can still be seen. The failing silk industry of the late 1700s was the inspiration for the birth of the economic boom of the 1800s when large mills were converted for cotton spinning. Inventions like the spinning jenny and the flying shuttle, aided by major advances in mechanical engineering, aided the rapid rise of this new textile industry. Hatting, an important trade from the mid 17th century onwards, flourished in the late 19th century with nearly 5,000 having employment in factories such as Christy's in late Victorian times. Stockport was once described as being 'one of the darkest and smokiest holes in the whole of the industrial area.' But, we know what they say in Yorkshire about muck and brass. New age technologies took over in the years between the world wars and different engineering companies altered both the way of life for locals and the skyline. Millgate Power Station, to the left, was one of the earliest of the newer developments. Built in 1898, it helped revolutionise people's lives. In Edwardian Stockport only 217 homes had electricity, but the demand for this marvellous harnessing of energy meant that the vast majority of houses had access by the late 1920s.

EVENTS OF THE 1950s

THE WORLD AT LARGE

Plans to develop the economies of member states into one common market came to fruition on 1st January 1958, when the EEC came into operation. The original members were France, Belgium, Luxembourg, The Netherlands, Italy, and West Germany. The Community became highly successful, achieving increased trade and prosperity across Western Europe while at the same time alleviating fear of war which lingered on after the end of World War II. Britain became a member in 1973.

ROYAL WATCH

King George VI's health had been causing problems since 1948, when he developed thrombosis. In 1951 the King - always a heavy smoker - became ill again, and was eventually found to be suffering from lung cancer. His left lung was removed in September of 1951. In January 1952 he waved Princess Elizabeth and Prince Philip off on their tour of Africa; they were never to see him again. The King died on 5th February 1952.

MELODY MAKERS

Few teenage girls could resist the blatant sex-appeal of 'Elvis the Pelvis', though their parents were scandalised at the moody Presley's provocatively gyrating hips. The singer took America and Britain by storm with such hits as 'Jailhouse Rock', 'All Shook Up' and 'Blue Suede Shoes'. The rhythms of Bill Haley and his Comets, Buddy Holly, Chuck Berry, and Roy Orbison (who had a phenomenal three-octave voice) turned the 1950s into the Rock 'n' Roll years.

Wartime

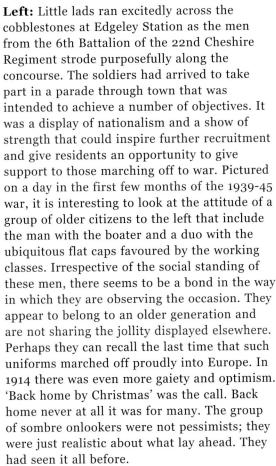

Left: Little lads ran excitedly across the cobblestones at Edgeley Station as the men from the 6th Battalion of the 22nd Cheshire Regiment strode purposefully along the concourse. The soldiers had arrived to take part in a parade through town that was intended to achieve a number of objectives. It was a display of nationalism and a show of strength that could inspire further recruitment and give residents an opportunity to give support to those marching off to war. Pictured on a day in the first few months of the 1939-45 war, it is interesting to look at the attitude of a group of older citizens to the left that include the man with the boater and a duo with the ubiquitous flat caps favoured by the working classes. Irrespective of the social standing of these men, there seems to be a bond in the way in which they are observing the occasion. They appear to belong to an older generation and are not sharing the jollity displayed elsewhere. Perhaps they can recall the last time that such uniforms marched off proudly into Europe. In 1914 there was even more gaiety and optimism. 'Back home by Christmas' was the call. Back home never at all it was for many. The group of sombre onlookers were not pessimists; they were just realistic about what lay ahead. They had seen it all before.

Above: A brass band led the way down Greek Street as members of the 6th Battalion 22nd Cheshire Regiment paraded in the autumn of 1939. It was only a few weeks ago when, on Sunday 3 September, Prime Minister Neville Chamberlain uttered the chilling words 'This country is at war with Germany' when there was no response to this country's ultimatum to Hitler to quit his assault on Poland.

Only the most supreme of optimists had thought otherwise, but a tingle ran down the spine when Chamberlain's words made it official. Britain had already begun mobilising its troops in anticipation of the inevitability of war. On the home front, some civil defence groups had been established and practised their responses to air raids. Children were prepared for evacuation from large towns and the nation waited with bated breath for what lay ahead. Emergency measures were immediately introduced. Householders were instructed to observe a strict blackout and homes were issued with stirrup pumps and shovels to deal with incendiary bombs that were expected any minute. Some regulations were very petty. People were told to carry a luggage label with their own name and address on it. Whether or not this was in case a body had to be sent home correctly tagged after an air raid has never been made clear. In the meantime, our boys paraded along the streets in a show of strength and were waved off to war by onlookers whose mood swung from pride to anxiety.

'Come friendly bombs and rain on Slough', John Betjeman once wrote in a critical description of the Berkshire town. He would have thought better of such flippancy had he been standing in Montagu Road in Offerton on 2 October 1940. At the time, these houses were relatively new, but the blast damage from the high explosives dropped during that first bombing raid to hit the town wrecked many of the homes that had only been in the possession of families for a few years. Remarkably, most were capable of being repaired and, though it took a while, the area was able to rise from the ashes. During the attack, eight large bombs and a host of incendiaries fell upon this district and Portwood, Hillgate, Cheadle Heath and Heaton Moor. Four people lost their lives in Marland Street, where most of the houses were destroyed. This assault on Stockport was just the prelude to a series of bombing raids mounted by the Luftwaffe on Stockport and its

environs. The air raid sirens sounded with increasing regularity on the run up to Christmas that year. On 22 and 23 December, incendiary bombs showered down. Only the sterling work of the emergency services, putting the safety of others before their own, saved the day and prevented Stockport becoming an uncontrollable inferno. The town was also unlucky enough to be the only one in the north hit by a doodlebug, a V-1 rocket.

Above: There are an unusual number of youngish men in this photograph of a Victory in Europe (VE Day) celebration. Most images of this sort were almost completely dominated by women, children and old men as the majority of dads and elder brothers were on active service. Possibly, these chaps were in some form of reserved occupation, vital for the war effort, and were able to join their families for the festivities that began on the morning of 8 May 1945 when word came through that General Jodl, the German Army Chief of Staff, had signed the instrument of surrender the previous day. By lunchtime, large crowds assembled in the capital to await the official announcement. Huge cheers went up when the Royal Family appeared and Winston Churchill also received a thunderous reception. The same sense of joy was expressed in humble backstreets across the country. These places were true communities. The residents lived, worked and played alongside one another. They shared the happiness of a family blessed by the birth of another child and helped out if someone ran short. There was also a strong bond in times of despair. During the war, when that dreadful telegram from the War Office was brought to the front door, everyone rallied round so that the mother or wife would not have to grieve alone.

Below: Children on School Street put on their best dresses and smartest short trousers to wave the flag in early May 1945. When news came through that Germany had surrendered, the whole country went potty. Giant congas were danced in the streets, pretty girls grabbed bobbies' helmets and paraded around with them set at a jaunty angle and anyone wearing a forces' uniform was grabbed and kissed unceremoniously. Almost every street in the land had its own VE Day party over the next few days. Rations were raided and cakes hurriedly baked using up what dried egg could be found. Spam sandwiches appeared by the dozen and watery jellies wobbled their way onto trestle tables purloined from churches and schoolrooms. Even the poorest communities had a sense of what was proper and tablecloths covered the trestles just as if rich Great Aunty Alice was coming to tea. Flags flew, bunting was waved and, in some cases, even bells form the Christmas decorations box kept in the attic were employed. We were used to making do after six years of turmoil. The parties were held for the children as they were our future. After all, had not their fathers gone off to the front to do battle in order that they should live in a world free from tyranny?

EVENTS OF THE 1940s

THE WORLD AT LARGE

The desert area of Alamogordo in New Mexico was the scene of the first atomic bomb detonation on July 16, 1945. With an explosive power equal to more than 15,000 tons of TNT, the flash could be seen 180 miles away. President Truman judged that the bomb could secure victory over Japan with far less loss of US lives than a conventional invasion, and on 6th August the first of the new weapons was dropped on Hiroshima. Around 80,000 people died.

ROYAL WATCH

By the end of World War II, the 19-year-old Princess Elizabeth and her distant cousin Lieutenant Philip Mountbatten RN were already in love. The King and Queen approved of Elizabeth's choice of husband, though they realised that she was rather young and had not mixed with many other young men. The engagement announcement was postponed until the Princess had spent four months on tour in Africa. The couple's wedding on 20th November 1947 was a glittering occasion - the first royal pageantry since before the war.

MELODY MAKERS

The songs of radio personalities such as Bing Crosby and Vera Lynn were whistled, sung and hummed everywhere during the 1940s. The 'forces' sweetheart' brought hope to war-torn Britain with 'When the Lights go on Again', while the popular crooner's 'White Christmas' is still played around Christmas time even today.

Who can forget songs like 'People Will Say we're in Love', 'Don't Fence Me In', 'Zip-a-dee-doo-dah', and 'Riders in the Sky'?

The lad in the foreground would be spanked quite soundly today for such a gesture. Then again, perhaps he wouldn't in our politically correct, nanny state society, though most normal folk think the opposite. However, in August 1945 the V sign had much greater significance than some form of silly, obscene comment. It represented the island nation that stood alone against the might of the Nazis during the war. Favoured by Winston Churchill, no less, the two fingered salute meant 'Victory' and we strove with all our might during those dark years to ensure that it came to pass. In truth, during the first half of the war we were more intent on survival, but that bulldog spirit and never say die attitude got us through. When hostilities ceased we partied like there was no tomorrow. In early May we had Victory in Europe (VE) Day and August brought us Victory in Japan (VJ) Day. Every street across the land was laden with goodies for the children as housewives used up their carefully hoarded rations to give the youngsters parties that they would never forget. Looking at this assembled throng, it is obvious that women and children dominate the scene. Most of the menfolk were still overseas. Sadly, many stayed there in cemeteries across the world that are a testament to a lost generation.

Events

Below: Hat making has been such an important industry in the making of modern Stockport that even the town's soccer team is known locally as 'The Hatters', though Luton Town fans might argue with the soubriquet. What cannot be disputed is the Hat Works Museum. Housed in Wellington Mill, once home to the Ward Brothers company, our town boasts Britain's only dedicated hat and hat making museum. It is a tribute to the work of such companies as Christy's, some of whose workers are seen here in 1937. These ladies were skilled in their art. Not every task could be performed by a machine as some parts of the process required specialist and delicate skills that could not be simulated by a lump of metal however well designed or programmed. Here the workers are involved in hat trimming. This involved tying the crown with gauze paper and then ironing it. Next, the lining and leather bindings were put into place. All of this was done by hand and the nimble fingers belonging to 1930s' women well used to darning, knitting and sewing at home were thought to be particularly suited to this type of work. It also meant that the bosses did not have to pay the sort of wages that they would have had to give to men performing such tasks.

Stetsons seem to be the headwear dominating the work of these ladies at Christy's Hat Works on Higher Hillgate. This just shows how much this company depended upon exports for its continued success. Not too many of the Cheshire set were likely to need such a fashion item as they made their way across the lawns at Bramall Hall or Lyme Park. Hat making is quite a lengthy process. Workers tended to specialise in one production area. Here we can see the trimmers taking a brief rest from their work. Elsewhere, you could find people treating the pelt in its initial phase along the journey to becoming a hat. There were forming and hardening stages as felting process continued. Blocking, shaping, dyeing, stiffening and weatherproofing all had their place before the final trimming touches were added and the finishing of the whole exercise achieved. In May 1937, the workforce was ready to celebrate the coronation of George VI. The former Duke of York was ill prepared for his onerous responsibility, having quite happily played second fiddle to his more outgoing elder brother who became Edward VIII in January 1936 after the death of their father, George V. When Edward abdicated in December, following the scandal of his liaison with Wallis Simpson, the nation prepared to welcome a different monarch. The new king was crowned on 12 May 1937, the date originally earmarked for his brother.

Above: One of the most popular figures of the last century visited Stockport on 22 June 1960. Born in 1900, Lady Elizabeth Angela Marguerite Bowes-Lyon, youngest daughter of the 14th Earl of Strathmore and Kinghorne, married Albert, Duke of York, in 1923. She was catapulted into major prominence in late 1936 when her husband replaced his brother as King, following the abdication crisis. He took the title of George VI and she became our Queen. Although a much loved figure in her own right, she became ever more popular in her role as Queen Mother after being widowed in 1952. So warmly did the public regard her that she rejoiced in the popular title of 'Queen Mum'. Locals turned out in their thousands to line the streets and enjoy a glimpse of the royal personage as she passed by. Looking south down Great Underbank today, the view of the shops is still much the same, though Boot's store is now a café and the Midland Bank has become the HSBC. The camera was pointed in the direction of the decorative timber framed Three Shires. This was once home to the Legh family of Adlington and dates from c1637. People out in force when the photograph was taken were more interested in the present than in ancient buildings and the town's streets were well bedecked with Union flags, both large and small.

Below: At the start of the swinging 60s there was little to suggest in the appearance of these young girls that some of them would be at the forefront of the sex, drugs and rock and roll revolution that was to come. In June 1960 most were just entering their teenage years and dressed as befitted the times. Their frocks and skirts were conventionally worn at just below knee length and many favoured white, ankle length socks, though a few of those who regarded themselves as being more mature had graduated to nylon stockings. By the end of the decade many would have become young housewives and mothers, but in the intervening years have moved away from fashions that their mothers had favoured. Mini skirts, kinky boots and Cathy McGowan hairstyles set them apart from the previous generation. On the day they were photographed outside Pullar's cleaners' shop and George Whitehead's stationery premises, the young ladies waited patiently for a glimpse of the Queen Mother as her motorcade went by. As they stood there they chatted about whether it was Don or Phil of the Everly Brothers that they preferred. But, girls are fickle and within a few years the decision would be between Paul and Ringo.

Below: Flags and bunting stretched across Great Underbank in 1960 for the visit of Elizabeth, the Queen Mother. Surprisingly, there did not seem to be any hand held ones on display. Normally, little flags on sticks were waved furiously during any royal visit, but no one seems to have bothered on this occasion. Looking north along the street towards the Union Bank, Lloyds Bank is now further along on the left and this site now occupied by Ladbroke's and Northern Rock. Property agents and an amusement arcade have replaced names such as the Woolwich and Seymour Mead, but the popularity of this area with the general public still persists. A royal visit always attracted large crowds, though they were generally dominated by women, as can be seen here. Housewives abandoned the shops for a while and it is lovely to see those fashions of nearly half a century ago. There are lots of floral designs on the summer dresses that, in many cases, billowed out below the knee over starched petticoats. The Queen Mother arrived in town at Edgeley Station and headed off to Christy's renowned hat making premises, but made sure that her route passed through the town centre where she gave her regal wave to the onlookers. Some had waited patiently for hours, but felt that the occasion warranted such a sacrifice.

Above: Stockport Town Hall was built in 1904-08 and is nicknamed 'the wedding cake' because of its particular Baroque style. Designed by Alfred Brumwell Thomas, it is the centrepiece of local administration and focal point for many important visitors. It was only natural that the Queen Mother should stop here during her visit in June 1960 and the crowds near the Town Hall steps were not disappointed when they caught sight of the royal visitor at close quarters. The sunny weather had persuaded most of the women in the picture to come into town without their hats or headscarves. Things were changing, because it was still a little unusual for a lady to be out and about, bareheaded. Certainly, the older generation did not think that it was properly attired without some form of head covering. The atmosphere was very relaxed and the bobby and female sergeant knew that they were in for an easy ride on crowd duties. There were no such thing as security concerns, because everyone loved the good old 'Queen Mum' and the occasion was marked by good natured chat and, eventually, cheering when the special guest came into view. Who could have guessed that the 60 year old royal would continue to be a point of national interest into the next century? She outlived many of the younger ones seen in this photograph.

Above: Robinson Street was just one of those insignificant, northern streets of terraced houses, situated close to Alexandra Park. But, on 2 June 1953, rich man, poor man, beggar and thief all celebrated the most joyous event since VJ Day. Social status was immaterial as we were all equal subjects of our newly crowned Queen Elizabeth II, or at least we were for a day. The weather was disappointing and those few with a television will never forget the sight of Queen Salote of Tonga as she headed for Westminster Abbey. This huge woman's beaming smile never faltered as her carriage slowly filled with rainwater. Elsewhere, there were street parties that went on all day. Children literally waved the flag and there was a picture of the young monarch in many front windows. Some of these children, perhaps grandparents by now, still have the coronation mugs and five shilling crowns that they were given at school or bought for them by a close relative. Can anyone believe that Charles and Camilla memorabilia will have such enduring qualities? In the early 1950s we lived in hope that this was to be the dawn of a new Elizabethan age. Rationing was still with us, in part, and the austerity of the immediate postwar era had hit hard. Perhaps a fresh face at Buckingham Palace was an omen for a better future.

Right: They say that air travel is the safest form of transport that there is, in comparison with the roads, rail and sea. Whether or not this is true, there is always something dramatic about an air crash, mainly because the number of casualties is likely to be high in any single incident. Sunday, 4 June 1967 saw some local residents making their way to church for the weekly service. Some prepared to have a run out to the seaside or merely decided to get out the lawnmower and tend to the garden. Others finished off a leisurely breakfast and turned to look at the newspaper to catch up on the previous day's events and cricket reports. There were also soccer stories about Glasgow Celtic fans still to return from celebrations in Lisbon after the team lifted the European Cup 10 days earlier, but there was another one that interested some readers. A DC-4 plane, owned by Air Ferry, carrying 83 holidaymakers home from the Costa Brava crashed in the Pyrenees, killing all on board. Just as that news was being digested, at 10 am a British Midland Argonaut carrying 84 passengers and crew on a holiday flight home from Majorca began its descent to Ringway Airport. Captain Harry Marlow reported 'trouble with the rpms' in a comment to air traffic control. As the aircraft continued to lose height and became unstable, Marlow knew that it was doomed. With a remarkable display of coolness under pressure, he was able to keep enough control of the plane to be able to guide it away from the most densely populated areas. Somehow, he brought it down in open ground near Stockport centre. Though badly injured, Captain Marlow survived, along with 11 others. Thankfully, there were no casualties on the ground.

Below: In 1953, Blackpool and Bolton contested what became known as 'the Matthews' final' when Stan finally got his winner's medal. But, 10 October was nearly half a year on from that game and the Edgeley Park mud a far cry from the lush turf at Wembley that had claimed yet another victim when Bolton's Eric Bell was hurt early on in the match. People tend to forget that when eulogising about Matthews' dribbling and Mortensen's goals. Whatever the events in London, the First Division giants who played there the previous May were light years away from Stockport County and Workington who met in this Third Division North clash. The visitors had only been a league side for two years and applied for re-election at the end of both seasons. Despite a 2-0 victory for County, Workington finished the season comfortably above the drop zone, thanks to the inspirational work of a young manager who was destined for the top, a certain Bill Shankly. Stockport's victory on this occasion was cemented by this goal from Jack Connor. Jack was a goal machine, notching 140 goals for the club in just 217 appearances. Coincidentally for the visiting team, Connor scored five times in one match against Workington. A much travelled footballer, he played for Ipswich, Carlisle, Rochdale and Bradford City before moving to Edgeley Park in 1951. He left for Crewe in 1956 after falling out with manager Willie Moir. Jack died in 1998, aged 78.

Above: Footballers had long been accustomed to wearing baggy, knee length shorts and heavy boots cared for by copious applications of Dubbin. With the increasing influence of television into their world and the interests of advertising gurus to satisfy, soccer started to take a note of fashion. Although stars such as Johnny Haynes had been feted as a Brylcreem Boy, it was the likes of George Best who moved footballers from the back pages of newspapers and into the gossip columns and news slots. Stockport County may not have been at the forefront of media interest, but the playing kit took some note of modern trends. The briefer shorts resembled something that Mary Quant might have designed, tracksuit tops had a stylish look and playing footwear became more streamlined. In the wake of England's successful 1966 World Cup campaign, attendances leapt at Football League grounds during the following season. County was one of the beneficiaries of the rekindled interest, particularly as it had a winning team. Just before the final match of the 1966-67 season at home to Lincoln City on 26 May, the lads held aloft the 4th Division championship trophy that was already theirs. Under the successful guidance of manager Jimmy Meadows, a former Manchester City fullback who had been one of many Wembley hoodoo victims when he was injured in the 1955 Cup Final, County was on its way to Division 3. Skipper Matt Woods is seen here being hoisted aloft. He had also witnessed the Wembley jinx at first hand when playing for Blackburn Rovers in 1960. Team mate Dave Whelan, later to be the financial force behind JJB Sports and Wigan Athletic, was stretchered off in the days before substitutes were allowed.

Shopping spree

The west side of Stockport market, seen in 1949, was in full swing. Such names as 'Sid's stall' has a lovely, homely ring to it. After the war, with rationing of some commodities still in force, housewives were anxious to do the best for their families on a restricted budget that was further limited by availability. Clothing and sweets only came off the list during this year. We might have won the war, but many grumbled that we were losing the peace. The threat of communism loomed large as the Berlin blockade continued, Mao Tse Tung took control in China and the Russians carried out an A-bomb test. The British Empire was falling apart and Eire and India both became republics. To cap it all, the pound was devalued by 30 per cent and everyone shook his head and wondered quite how such a once great nation could so quickly have become an also ran behind the new super powers of the USSR and the USA. Whilst doing their shopping, Stockport folk could at least look back on some fine traditions associated with their town that dated back many years. The fine Market Hall, where they found lots of bargains, has its links with Norman times when charters were granted to hold a weekly market and annual fair. The present iron and steel building was erected in 1861 and the interior has a light and airy feel to it, thanks to the large amount of glass that was used in its construction. Originally, the sides were open and the nickname of 'the glass umbrella' was born. The hall was fully enclosed in the late 1890s just after the time when a certain Ephraim (Michael) Marks ran a stall here. He teamed up with Thomas Spencer in Leeds and a new retailing story was born.

EVENTS OF THE 1940s

WHAT'S ON?

In wartime Britain few families were without a wireless set. It was the most popular form of entertainment, and programmes such as ITMA, Music While You Work and Workers' Playtime provided the people with an escape from the harsh realities of bombing raids and ration books. In 1946 the BBC introduced the Light Programme, the Home Service and the Third Programme, which gave audiences a wider choice of listening.

GETTING AROUND

October 1948 saw the production of Britain's first new car designs since before the war. The Morris Minor was destined for fame as one of the most popular family cars, while the four-wheel-drive Land Rover answered the need for a British-made off-road vehicle.

The country was deeply in the red, however, because of overseas debts incurred during the war. The post-war export drive that followed meant that British drivers had a long wait for their own new car.

SPORTING CHANCE

American World Heavyweight Boxing Champion Joe Louis, who first took the title back in 1937, ruled the world of boxing during the 1930s and 40s, making a name for himself as unbeatable. Time after time he successfully defended his title against all comers, finally retiring in 1948 after fighting an amazing 25 title bouts throughout his boxing career. Louis died in 1981 at the age of 67.

Below: Courting couples, friends out shopping or just pals getting together would often arrange to meet under Winter's clock. It still is a distinctive feature of Stockport's architectural heritage and continues to be used by some as a handy reference or meeting point. Little Underbank is a delightful part of town, full of character and with a real feel of yesteryear about it. In 1955, cars bowled along here making life difficult for pedestrians, but today it is much easier to take in the sights and history along here. Winter's clock indicates the business begun by Jacob Winter in 1859. He was a multi talented individual, being a watch and clockmaker, silversmith, optician and jeweller. The name above the door is still the same, but now Joseph Holt's ales are dispensed from the premises. The delightfully wrought bridge, St Petersgate, was also known as Angel Bridge, after the Market Place pub of that name. Designed by Rawlinson and built by Pierce, it opened on 24 February 1868 and cost £10,500. Stockport's coat of arms is incorporated into the structure. Our armorial bearings were granted on 5 December 1932. They show the shield of arms belonging to the De Stokeport family, with other elements derived from arms borne by the Earl of Chester, the De Eatons, the De Warrens and the Earl of Derby. Supporting lions were added in 1960.

The town motto 'Animo et Fide' translates as 'With courage and faith'.

Right: In 1680, the largest corn mill in the manor was to be found here on what was formerly Milne Gate. Stand at the top of Millgate today, in between Market Hall and St Mary's Church, and the view down the brow is not the one that we have here from the late 1960s. Neither half timbered building nor cooling tower belonging to the power station catches the eye. Instead, we now gaze down upon the back entrance to Asda, hardly a nostalgic image that anyone in the 21st would wish to snap. Some 40 years ago, two of the younger market traders seem to have taken a few minutes out to have a little chat. What can we read into their body language? Is her pose, with head cocked to one side, slightly coquettish or does the arm across her chest suggest a defensive attitude? Her companion is slightly unsure of himself, rocking backwards as he tries to make an impression. These were the swinging 60s, but some things never change. Men may have made the running, but it has always been the women who called the shots. Oh the power of the femme so very fatale! The building above the stall sold wallpaper at the knockdown price of 3s 3d or 3s 11d a roll. That is 16p or 20p at today's prices. A firm of solicitors now occupy the premises.

Prince Edward, Earl of Chester, granted a market charter in 1260. This formal declaration gave legitimacy to an already established practice and was indicative of the town's increasing legitimacy as a commercial centre. Initially, Thursday was allocated as market day and, ever since then, Stockport market has thrived. This scene from c1965 shows the Produce Hall, to the right. It was built in 1852 on the site of Stockport's first Post Office and was also known as the Hen Market or Cheese Hall. What was at one time a library on the first floor is now a café, but the hall still provides an opportunity for shoppers to buy fresh produce. Although names such as Chafes, London Scottish, Town Warden and New Image now decorate the ground floor facades of the buildings on this side of Market Place, the main fabric of the buildings is largely unaltered and lends a stylish feel to this part of town. The classical style of the Corinthian columns on the Produce Hall is particularly noteworthy. They alone cost £4,200, a princely sum in the middle of the 19th century. But, their aesthetic value is immeasurable. Who can say that about some of the concrete, steel and glass monstrosities foisted upon us in the 1970s by so called architects and planners? What is sure is that their constructions will soon be gone and little lamented and never match the 150 plus years, and still counting, of the Produce Hall's existence.

From school to work

Left: What a lovely sight and does it not warm the cockles of even the most hardened of hearts? The children enjoying the sunshine, if they are still with us today, will be in their late 70s as this photograph was taken during the 1930s. That was a decade of depression, with up to 3 million out of work and hunger marches on London and rioting in the streets a not uncommon sight. Yet, for these tots there was a chance for a brief escape from the harsh realities of life before the war. They were off to the seaside for the day. Faces brightly scrubbed and knees nicely cleaned, mums got them dressed in their best bib and tucker turnout for their treat. Although history does not relate where they were off to, somewhere like Blackpool or Rhyl would have been top of the agenda. Packed into a motor coach, or 'chara' as we used to call it, the children were whisked along the road towards their destination. The journey would take at least two hours as motorways had not been thought of, but that did not matter. They knew what was in store at the end of the journey. There were donkeys to be ridden, Punch and Judy shows to see, sandcastles to be built and the sea to be paddled in. There was ice cream to be guzzled and a good sleep to be had on the way back, at least for those who weren't being sick.

Above: Woodworking classes were part of the curriculum for boys seen here in the workshop of the Stockport Technical and Art School about a century ago. Even now, many of us can relate to our own schooldays when we were instructed in the art of using vices, chisels, planes and tenon saws. How proud we were when we added the finishing touches to the ink stand or letter rack we had made. Sitting rooms across the country were littered with such items that lads brought home, the fruit of their labours. They were given pride of place alongside the embroidered place mats and scarves their sisters had produced. These were the days when girls and boys followed different strands in their handicraft lessons. Young ladies did not need to learn about spirit levels or tongue and groove flooring and it was infra dig for any red blooded male to be seen with a pair of knitting needles or crochet hook. In 1886, Sir Joseph Leigh, Mayor of Stockport, suggested the founding of a technical school as the textile industry was suffering from increased competition from abroad. Young people, coached in the new technology of modern design and production, were needed to address the overseas challenge. The school opened in 1889 with 1,000 students on roll for both day and evening classes. It was the forerunner of the College of Further and Higher Education.

Above: Crumbs! We hope not, as this forklift truck was loading boxes of McVitie biscuits onto a lorry at the despatch department. The picture is from the 1950s, by which time the biscuit factory had been well established in Stockport and the company was a household name. Dunking a Rich Tea, sucking on a Chocolate Digestive and picking up a Penguin became part of the nation's culture as McVitie's built up to a mammoth 25 per cent of the country's biscuit market. The company story began in Scotland when, in 1830, Robert McVitie established a small bakery in an Edinburgh tenement house. The quality of his baking soon established a formidable reputation, especially when helped by the commercial nous of Charles Price, an eventual partner with a keen eye for marketing. From 1888 the firm was known as McVitie and Price and, although the latter partner left in 1901 to enter Parliament as a Liberal MP, the dual company name was still in use. It came to Stockport in 1917 as part of the war effort. To think that a biscuit company as well as a munitions factory could play a significant role in helping beat the enemy might seem incongruous at first. But, as Napoleon is reputed to have said, an army marches on its stomach. What were known as 'iron rations', in fact plain biscuits, were needed to supplement the dietary needs of those at the front and the Stockport factory supplied what was required.

Above: Tangy, sherbet roundels and refreshing, circles of Love Hearts are the main products we associate with the Swizzels company. This lorry from the 1950s had a twofold use as a courier and advertising platform. The bold picture and slogan on the side left little need for further explanation. The business began during a difficult time for anyone attempting a new venture. Post first world war Britain was a time of economic depression when Londoners Alf and Maurice Matlow set up a sweets and confectionery business. They teamed up with David Dee in 1933 to form Swizzels and hit on the idea of sweets in compressed tablet form. Their fizzy style of goods was almost unique and soon gained popularity in a niche few could challenge.

Various lines were manufactured, with Parma Violets, Fruit Fizzers and Refreshers being amongst the most popular. However, Love Hearts are possibly the favourite amongst these sweets. The circular tablets with the heart shape on top always contain a short, happy message. 'Smile', 'I'm yours' 'Hug me' etc were all meant to make someone smile, or perhaps cringe. The company relocated to New Mills during the blitz of the second world war. Several generations of youngsters have been brought up to appreciate the fizzing sensation on the tongue when a Swizzels' product hits the taste buds. Parents secretly enjoy them and are only too happy to accept one of the firm's sweets when offered by a generous child.

Above: White coats lend an air of the scientific to the work of these ladies hard at work at their benches. This is quite an accurate assessment of what was being undertaken as they had to carry out their tasks with precision and efficiency. They were part of the workforce that originally produced sophisticated goods from premises in a converted furniture factory in School Street, Hazel Grove for what is now known as Philips Semiconductors. Formerly Salford Electrical Instruments, the company was to become part of GEC and opened an additional factory at Broadstone Mill in Reddish. There was a further name change to Associated Semiconductor Manufacturers in 1962 and it was taken over by Mullards, once just a radio valve company, in 1969. The following year saw a move to Pepper Road, Hazel Grove, though the Philips name was not adopted until 1988. Women made good workers in this specialised field as they generally possessed greater dexterity than their male counterparts and were better suited to the intricate nature of quite a lot of the work. Their working conditions were a far cry from those their mothers and grandmothers might have experienced in the cotton mills. There was good lighting and an airy atmosphere for them to work in, as could be proved by the number of birds who managed to fly in and out of the rafters.

Below: This raised view of the huge shop floor of the company that was to become known as Philips Semiconductors shows row after row of mainly female workers on task as they carefully assembled the items that once were valves but later became silicon chips. Such large factory floors gave rise to a camaraderie that went well beyond the workplace. Young women forged friendships that would last a lifetime. In the 1950s, long before this photograph was taken, they chatted over their work about boyfriends and the latest double feature they were going to see on Saturday night at the 'flicks'. They also listened intently to 'Workers' Playtime', that daily dose of radio variety that brought them popular tunes and turns by comedians such as Arthur 'hello playmates' Askey or Ken 'I won't take my coat off' Platt. Managers realised that a happy shop floor was a productive one and a grin on a girl's face after one of cheeky chappie Max Miller's risqué gags was likely to achieve an increase in productivity. Eventually, such radio broadcasts were phased out, especially when the BBC scrapped the old light, home and third services and ushered in Radio 1,2,3 and 4. A non stop stream of pop music became the fare, but it lacked the individuality of the old entertainment.

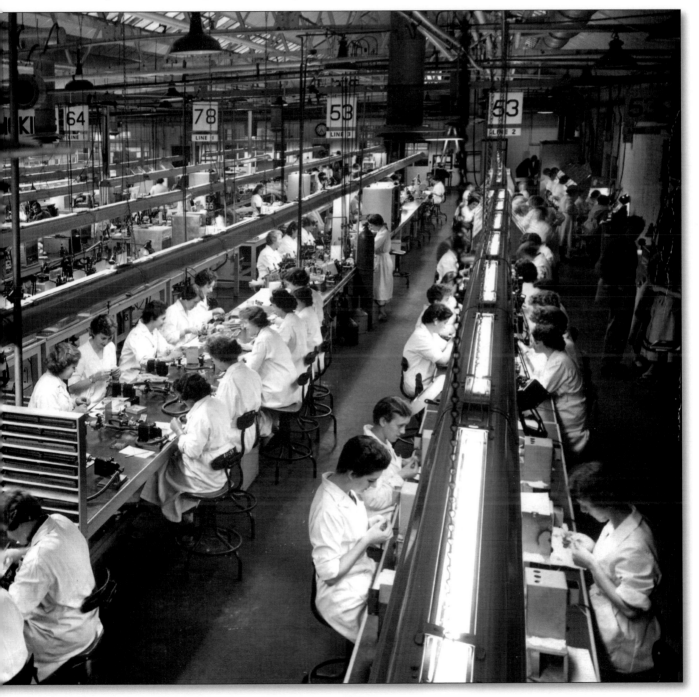

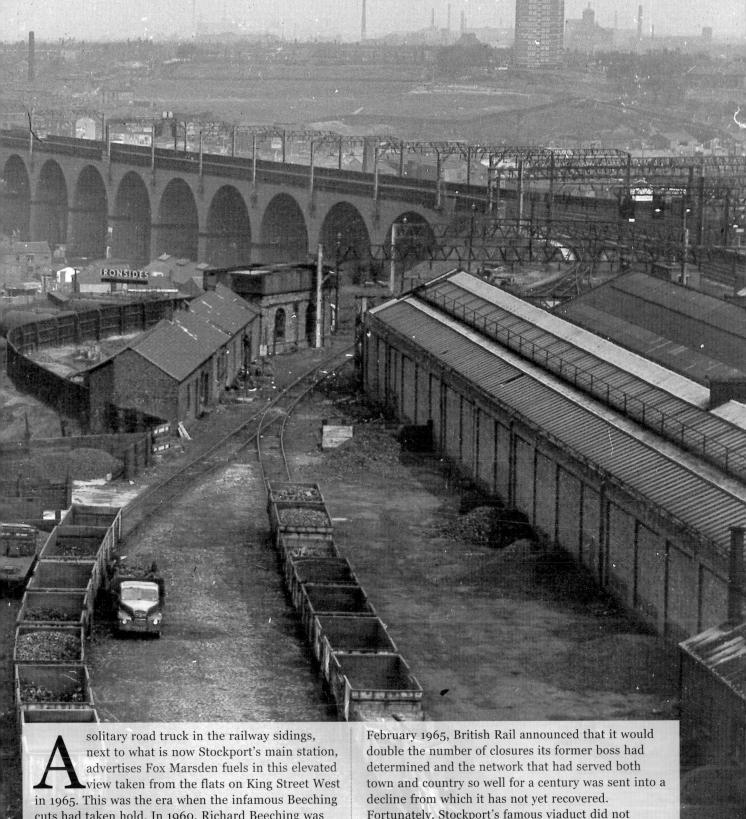

A solitary road truck in the railway sidings, next to what is now Stockport's main station, advertises Fox Marsden fuels in this elevated view taken from the flats on King Street West in 1965. This was the era when the infamous Beeching cuts had taken hold. In 1960, Richard Beeching was appointed to head a four man inquiry into the state of the railway system. He became the head of British Railways the following year. In 1963 his report recommended the closing of over 2,000 stations, axing many branch lines and reducing the rail network by a quarter. Having been allowed to do his worst, the now Lord Beeching was sacked at the end of 1964. In February 1965, British Rail announced that it would double the number of closures its former boss had determined and the network that had served both town and country so well for a century was sent into a decline from which it has not yet recovered. Fortunately, Stockport's famous viaduct did not feature in any closure plans. The huge construction is one of the north of England's most impressive testaments to the vision and workmanship of the early Victorians. Built in 1840, it consists of 27 arches and contains 11 million bricks in its one third of a mile span. Architect John Lowe and engineer George W Buck left Stockport a marvellous legacy.

European Colour

The world would be a dull drab place without colour in it. A Stockport firm which knows more about colour than most is EC Pigments based in Hempshaw Lane.

In historic terms the name EC Pigments is relatively modern, but the firm traces its local roots back to the reign of Queen Victoria.

Today memories are fading of Ellis Jones & Co Ltd. That company was established in 1877 in Manchester by Ellis Jones who was the second son of Edward Jones a calico printer. Ellis was a partner in James Black & Co of Dalmanach Print Works.

In 1880 John W Spence formed a chemical manufacturing company in Glasgow under the name of John W Spence & Co. Four years later John Spence married Ellis Jones's sister. That marriage eventually led to the merging of the businesses of Ellis Jones and J.W.Spence though the business continued to operate using the two separate trade names.

Ellis Jones died in 1893 but his younger brother, E. Fielding Jones joined J.W Spence & Co as a partner.

Fielding Jones and John Spence, along with a James Wilkinson, now set up a company the Providence Drysalters Company.

Top left: Mr Alf Folds inside the Ellis Jones lab circa 1928.
Above right: An early view inside the works Colour Lab.
Right: Ellis Jones own transport with side inscription: Pulp Colours Satin White.

E.F. Jones became the manager of the new enterprise's American branch.

The partnership was dissolved in 1909 and John W Spence became the sole proprietor of Ellis Jones & Co, which by then had moved to Stockport.

On 3rd December 1923 Ellis Jones & Co (Stockport)Ltd became a private limited company, with the name of its two subscribers listed as John William Spence of Darley House, West Didsbury and Ellis Edward Spence of Ardlui, Alderley Edge.

market. British industry then began to manufacture for UK requirements. These were sodium salts of Lithol Red, Lake Red C and Rubine 2B & 4B types of dyes. The Barium and Calcium salts of these dyes were sold as reduced forms on suitable extenders.

The Dyestuff Act of 1920 prohibited importation of any dyestuff which could be satisfactorily made in the United Kingdom. Toners were also included in the prohibition.

As a result of the 1920 Act there was a large increase in the production of reds, like 'Toluidines', 'Perm Red', '2B', '4B' and 'Lithol Types'.

For many years the telegraphic address of Ellis Jones & Co would be ARDLUI.

John W Spence died in 1924 and his widow became Chairman of the company, a position she would hold until her death in 1950.

The early days of the Company were developed on an Oil Business. In this field there is no doubt that it was a world leader in many aspects. i.e. Sulphated Oils-Castor-Sperm-Fish-Linseed, along with soluble cutting oil bases.

Prior to the first world war, the British pigment industry was based on formulations handed down from father to son. However, from then on it became a more technically controlled industry, one in which the chemist was now king.

Until then, inorganic chemical compounds had been at the forefront of the industry, with lead chromes, greens, Prussian blue and ultramarine. Reds, other than oxides, were 'Lakes' and 'Madders'.

Pigment dyestuffs were imported from Germany, these flooded the

Lake Colours from acid dyestuffs were largely used for paper coating and transparent printing ink colours.

'P.M.T.A.' Toners appeared around this time. Before this Arsenical and Tannic Lakes were used for bright colours.

Top left: *General view of Tiviot Colour Works from Canal Basin.* **Below:** *Pulp colour casks.*

In the 1930s 'Phthalocyanine Blue' was introduced. This was a major discovery to the pigment colour field: being of British origin this enhanced the standing of the UK industry.

Demand for zinc chromes as lead-free anti-corrosive pigment grew as the second world war drew nearer.

During the war, efforts were directed towards government requirements. Camouflage colours were in large demand. Pigment Green B, Ultramarine, Earth colours, Yellow Ochre and Red Oxide were the main requirements. But for identification purposes, bright colours were required: orange for dinghies, zinc chromes for aircraft and colours for cable identification.

There was of course rationing of raw materials, which the BCMA. devised and ran with government approval. It also rationalised the number of chrome greens to avoid waste of materials and labour which would otherwise have occurred.

Ellis Jones expanded into colour beginning with simple Lake Colours with particular reference to the paper-coating Industry.

Many hundreds of tons of 'Cadbury Violet', 'Rowntree Red' and 'Rizla Orange & Green' were supplied to the paper-coating industry, where many

Above: Water Storage above Well Head.
Below: Pigment vats at Tiviot Colour Works.

manufacturers had contracts for each shade which were 'Friction Glazed' to obtain satisfactory results. With the development of printing inks, 'Gloss' became more important. Ultimately more and more wrappers were developed with gloss during printing rather than by the previous paper-coating methods.

Another large production in the early days was with 'Satin White', again for high quality white paper coatings, with particular use as base paper for the production of postage stamps.

The company also had a large business with Hayes Mill in providing Lakes devised with special properties required for Record Labels. Hayes Mill was situated next door to the EMI record factory in Hayes, Middlesex.

Another very large outlet for the company's production in those days was for 'Dispersion of Carbon Black' for

Above: The entrance of Tiviot Colour Works, the original site on Manchester Road. Left: Rescued at last! by H Astington and A Folds, 1947.

the production of what was known as the 'Mill Board Industry'.

Two companies in particular were major customers: Jacksons Millboard and Western Board Mills. Ellis Jones supplied hundreds of 40 gallon drums of its 'Dispersion' to be used in the coloration of Dark Grey Millboard.

In those days the millboard was used for the formation of motor car dashboards, door panels and laundry boxes.

Another field in which Ellis Jones led the industry was with highly reduced pigments for use in scholastic powder colour paints.

The company produced these products on 'Edge Runners', where say, 90% 'extender' with pigment would yield a standard which when used by the paint manufacturer, would still look like red rather than a pink when this was opened by the teacher in school.

Many hundreds of tons were supplied to major scholastic colour manufacturers in this form for many years until they improved their own dispersion techniques.

In the first 50 years of the BCMA however the complexity of organic pigments increased enormously with increasing acceleration since. For example, between 1956 and 1966 the Colour Index listed an increase in chemically different organic pigments from 316 to 454.

Top: An aerial view of the site, circa 1970s.
Above: Celebrating the company's centenary, April 1977.

At the time of the BCMA's Golden Jubilee, it was felt that far more sophisticated organic chemistry would be needed in the future. Further, because of unattractive factories, the colour pigment industry was falling behind in the recruitment race for plant operators and supervisors of the right calibre. A prediction was made that there would be a decline in the number of pigment manufacturing companies as smaller companies merged into fewer larger units.

In 1977 Ellis Jones employees celebrated 100 years in business at Mottram Hall in Prestbury. Yet there were dark clouds on the horizon.

During the early 1980s the company was faced with some difficult choices. Ellis Jones had invested heavily in a new pigment plant in the late 1970s (a conversion of a brewery on Hempshaw Lane) but with weak demand in the industry, a high level of gearing and products steadily falling behind market needs, the business had to restructure to survive.

Restructuring meant significant debt reduction from internal sources, and sadly the oils division, and subsequently the original site, were sold. A new management team then set about revitalising each area of the business: stabilising product quality, increased production efficiency, reducing order lead times, developing new products and pushing sales into continental Europe.

There then followed a strong recovery in the company's performance and in 1988 the company effected a reverse takeover of Horace Cory Plc, another long established pigment company based in Woolwich, London.

The Woolwich site produced a similar range of pigments to the Stockport plant but with the addition of synthetic food colours and also dye complex pigments which were toll manufactured for a multinational pigment maker.

In 1994 the company bought the dye complex pigment business from Ciba pigments and with improved products and increased marketing, the sales volume on this range was increased three-fold.

By the late 1990s European Colour was selling to over 50 countries world wide. The only market that still proved difficult to penetrate was the USA, and in 1999 European Colour acquired the US company Roma Color based in Fall River, Massachusetts. This acquisition gave European Colour (t/a EC Pigments) manufacturing, marketing and distribution capabilities within three major global market areas: North America, Europe and Asia.

Over recent years the pigment industry and its customers, (in ink, paint and plastics production) have seen tremendous downward pressure on prices as low cost product has flooded the markets from Asia. As a result EC Pigments has had to re-position itself and focus more and more on the speciality areas of the pigments business. The culture of the business is obsessive about its customers and quality. It is market driven and continues to be international in its outlook with research and development playing a key role in the future success of the business.

Left: *A view inside one of the many EC Pigments labs.*
Above: *R&D heads and Scientific Advisory Board - 2005.*

AG Parfett

Few businesses manage to grow from almost nothing to having sales of hundreds of millions of pounds a year in just 25 years. Of those which do, fewer still can have survived a disastrous fire or faced the destruction of much of their stock in their first year. One firm which has triumphed over such enormous difficulties to make itself one of the most important enterprises not only in Stockport but in the whole region is Parfetts, the family wholesaling firm.

It was in July 1980 that AG Parfett & Sons Ltd, the cash & carry company, based in Didsbury Road began trading. The firm was founded by Alan Parfett and his wife Pat together with their eldest son Steve, originally operating from a 25,000 sq ft warehouse in Reddish. The couple's youngest son Robert joined the company in 1981. Daughters Barbara and Judy too have also worked for the firm with great success.

Alan Parfett had worked for various food companies since 1945 and had often thought of setting up in business for himself. The opportunity came in 1979 when a cash and carry unit in Reddish came on the market. Together with his family he decided to start the family business.

A staff member, who already worked at the warehouse when the Parfetts arrived, recalls that the existing staff were a little apprehensive because the place was very disorganised and there were hardly any customers. That apprehension was clearly misplaced: the family had big plans and things improved quickly; all of a sudden staff actually had customers and things to do! Linda Livesey, one of those first employees, who is still employed by Parfetts, recalls that being a family business meant everyone was required to help out in those early days. It was not unusual to see both Pat and Alan Parfett helping out with the cleaning up and making those ever important cups of tea.

Top left: *Founders Alan and Pat Parfett.*
Below: *Parfett's original warehouse in Reddish pictured in 1982.*

But it was not plain sailing. Shortly after opening the doors Parfetts became victims of an Australian spider beetle infestation which meant the warehouse having to be closed down for an entire weekend with friends and family pitching in to help clear infected stock. The loss of sales and stock cost over £5,000. At the end of that first year however the firm had still managed to make a profit of £500. Perhaps not a lot but enough to encourage the family which had not expected to see any profit.

Hard work however eventually began to pay off. That did not mean they changed their economical ways however. When Pat Parfett noticed furniture missing from her house she didn't worry about burglars; she simply knew that Alan had been taking it to fill the ever expanding needs of the company office.

By 1983 the Reddish depot had become one of the busiest wholesale cash and carry outlets in the UK.

An extension of another 15,000 sq ft was added in 1984 making the depot Manchester's premier cash and carry business. Disaster however, struck in December 1986 when a fire destroyed the warehouse.The blaze which had been started by children playing in a skip took eleven fire engines to extinguish.

Alan Parfett was woken at 4 am by his son Robert to be given the bad news. Robert and Steve had been there all night, having themselves been told of the blaze by long-standing employee Lynda Livesey who had received a call from her brother saying the depot was on fire. Lynda had looked out of her bedroom window and seen the flames for herself. In the morning staff arrived to discover a terrible mess, they had to wear wellington boots, and went home smelling of smoke, but they did what needed to be done. It could have been the end but the Parfetts made sure no one even lost a day's pay. Alan went to the office and assured the employees that their jobs were safe and that he would rebuild.

Such a disaster would break many firms, indeed they would break many individuals. The Parfett family did not despair as so many others might have done. With true northern grit they pulled themselves together, assessed the damage and decided what needed to be done. Fortunately both family members and their dedicated employees were up to the task.

Within fourteen weeks Parfetts was back in business in a new warehouse of 60,000 sq ft on Didsbury Road. Since then the Heaton Norris depot has had two extensions built bringing the total floor space to 100,000 sq ft.

Top: Another happy customer at Reddish cash and carry.

Parfetts bought a second warehouse unit in1986, this time at Liverpool. The new 82,000 sq ft depot was soon so successful that within five years it became inadequate and a new unit of 105,000 sq ft had to be built behind it at a cost of over £3 million.

In 1988 the company won the first of many industry awards by being given the Independent Cash and Carry of the Year Award presented by the Independent Grocer magazine, an award which the company would go on to receive for four consecutive years.

The following year a third unit, of 40,000 sq ft, was acquired in Anfield and extensively modernised.

In February 1989, after almost a decade at the helm, Alan Parfett retired becoming Chairman of the company whilst son Steve was appointed Managing Director, assisted by his brother Robert, responsible for personnel, IT and marketing and Financial Director Robert Miller.

Alan's parting advice to his sons was that they would need to achieve £100 million in sales in the tenth year - and they did.

In 1991 the company was featured in the Independent on Sunday as one of the top fifty fastest growing private companies in the UK; a reason for that was clear when the Stockport depot was voted Britain's No.1 Cash and Carry by off-licence retailers.

Parfetts acquired the 117,000 sq ft Watson & Philip cash and carry business in Somercotes, Derbyshire in 1994. The following year Steve Parfett became Chairman of Landmark, a voluntary wholesale group of which the firm had been an active member since being founded.

A fifth depot would be acquired in 1998 through the purchase of a fellow Landmark member's business in Halifax, where less than two years later sales were up by 50 per cent.

Meanwhile awards continued to be gained: in 1995 Andrew Kenny the firm's IT manager was awarded the FWD Gold medal for Information Technology Development. A year later the company was rated 49th out of 150 of the region's top companies in a Manchester Evening News survey. In 1997 John Chapman, the company Marketing Manager received the FWD President's Gold medal for outstanding services to the wholesale industry whilst in 1999 Peter Mullan General Manager of Parfetts

Below: *The aftermath of the fire at Reddish in 1986.*

Stockport received the FWD Gold Medal for Manager of the year.

In March 2000 Steve Parfett was elected Chairman of the Federation of Wholesale Distributors, a position his father had held in the 1980s.

The company has changed almost beyond recognition in the years since it was founded, and certainly surpassed its founder's expectations. However, its core business continues to be the sale of goods strictly to trade customers, whether they be retail grocers, off-licences or newsagents, or catering customers running cafes, hotels or pubs. Despite the fact that this customer base, particularly the independent retailers, have faced enormous pressure and competition from the supermarkets, Parfetts have succeeded in achieving growth in every one of its years in business.

In its first year of trading in 1980 the company had sales of £3 million and a staff of twelve; by 2000, the firm's twentieth year, the company had grown to a business which employed 400 staff in five stores and enjoyed an annual turnover in excess of £200 million.

Most recently a sixth store, in Sheffield has opened. Meanwhile awards and accolades continue to be earned - in both 2004 and 2005 for example the company won the

Cash and Carry of the Year Awards in the Harris International Marketing Awards, a particularly welcome recognition, being based on independent retailers' satisfaction with their wholesaler.

Alan Parfett's greatest hope in his retirement is that Parfetts will continue to grow steadily, and that one day his grandchildren will show an interest in joining the business ensuring that the firm continues to be a family concern.

Top: *Employee Dot Smith restocking the shelves in 1987.*
Above: *The Parfett Family pictured in November 2004.*

Chris Bennett - Haul the way

Got a heavy load to shift? If so you need Chris Bennett (Heavy Haulage) Ltd, specialists in the general and heavy haulage industry. The business was established in the mid 1970s as an 'owner-driver' operator with a single Ford 'D' series truck. The company has grown and developed over the years and now operates a modern mixed fleet of more than 40 vehicles. Today the company is one of the leading specialist in its field, providing a haulage service to some of the largest blue chip construction, engineering, plant hire, aviation, manufacturing and demolition companies across the United Kingdom.

The company is still family owned and family run. It takes great pride in providing the levels of service which can only be achieved by a company whose the directors are 'hands on' and have a full understanding of the business, its customers and its customers needs.

Operating from its depot in Stockport close to the motorway network enables the company to provide a comprehensive service throughout the UK, Ireland and Europe.

Staff at Stockport's Chris Bennett (Heavy Haulage) Ltd are often required to plan their journeys like a military campaign in order to avoid disaster and to minimise disruption for other roads users.

Most readers will have travelled on the motorways and seen slow moving orange flashing lights in the distance before eventually overtaking a vehicle flanked by police cars and carrying an extra wide load. It may be just a nuisance to the passing motorist but for those responsible for the huge load the job not only requires great skill and forethought but also provides the satisfaction which only comes from knowing that a difficult job has been well done.

Most jobs take up far more time in the planning than in the execution. Will a load pass under all the bridges

Top left: *Founder Chris Bennett.*
Below: *Chris Bennett about to embark in his early days of haulage whilst working for Keogh's of Wilmslow.*

Chris Bennett it has been the fulfilment of a dream.

Born in 1947 in Wilmslow, where he still lives, Christopher Harry Bennett was one of a family of twelve children. He had left school at the age of 15 to work in the building trade but left that job to become a driver's mate. After 10 years heavy haulage experience with Keoghs of Wilmslow Chris set up on his own in 1976

Chris' first vehicle was ELO 492J, a D Series Ford which came from Hertz Truck Rental and cost Chris £350. Once he had renovated the vehicle Chris used it to make collections and deliveries all over the country

on the proposed route? Are bends in the road wide enough for vehicles to negotiate them? Are police escorts available, and from which forces? Are any roadworks planned which might otherwise unexpectedly appear half way along the journey? How is the cargo to be unloaded at its destination? What is the back up plan in the event of a breakdown?

For most folk this degree of planning and the need for absolute attention to detail would be a nightmare. For

The business was run from a yard at the rear of Dean Print, Stockport Road, Cheadle Heath where it would remain until 1991.

Top: Chris Bennett's fist vehicle purchased in 1976.
Above: Chris Bennett alongside his second vehicle a Scammell Handyman, 1977.

Vehicle number two was a Scammel Handyman ETF 547J followed by JUT 893L.

Not many Leyland Clydesdale operated on the heavy haulage scene but Chris had five years service from his - operating up to 32 tons gross. The Clydesdale was originally coupled with a Taskers Little Giant low loader. Chris paid £3,500 for the outfit in 1978.

Chris Bennett Transport Ltd was formed in 1983. A265 HVM was its first 6x4 tractor, the DAF 3300 being rated for 125 tonnes gross. The unit was bought second hand and was first driven for Bennetts by Keith Small. Like the rest of the Bennett fleet the DAF was named after one of Chris relatives - in this case Lorraine his daughter.

Chris had bought his first DAF - YJP 670T in 1980. He liked the two year old vehicle so much that he stayed with the marque for many years afterwards.

After problems during the recession of the early 1990s Chris Bennett reformed his business operations in 1992 under the new name Chris Bennett (Heavy Haulage) Ltd. A fresh start prompted a change in livery

Right: Chris Bennett pictured in 1978.
Below: Chris Bennett's third vehicle in St Hellier, Jersey.

with M877 WKF being the first brand new tractor unit to sport the now familiar grey, red and white colours. The Leyland DAF 95-430 Space cab 6x4 unit was rated for 150 tonnes operation.

In 1991 the firm left its long-time base in Cheadle Heath and moved to its present premises at Arden Hall, Far Cromwell Road, Bredbury.

By then the Bennett fleet had grown to 30 strong - a mix of 7.5 tonners, crane equipped rigids as well as heavy haulage low loaders making larger premises an imperative.

From just one vehicle and its driver/owner in 1976 the firm now has a staff of 57: drivers, drivers mates,

workshop and franchise-trained technicians, fabricators and welders ensuring that the fleet of vehicles is kept on the move and that 'uptime' is kept to a maximum. The company operates a one truck driver policy. Drivers are trained to the highest standards and are all equipped with mobile communications. Vehicles are fitted with the latest satellite tracking facilities ensure that staff know exactly where clients' consignments are at any time of the day or night.

A customer service centre is open 24 hours a day seven days a week, manned by fully trained and experienced operators who are able to assist with any eventuality. The firm also has available both indoor and outdoor storage facilities as well as fork-lift equipment capable of off-loading up to 14 tonnes.

fitters - who were doing most of the company's own maintenance - and office staff.

Included in those staff numbers are Chris himself, daughter Lorraine who take care of the office, as well as sons Chris Junior and Anthony a heavy haulage driver and private escort vehicle driver respectively.

In 1976 Chris had set out buying a tractor unit for £350 plus two low loaders for £150 each. Now with 40 wagons, trailers and support vehicles available it's a sign of serious success when his latest acquisitions have been a Volvo 620 BHP tractor which cost £112,000 plus a seven axle low loader which cost £195,000.

Nor is that the only change: in 1976 turnover was just £22,000 by 2005 that figure had grown a hundred fold to over £4 million.

Most of the vehicles are 'franchise maintained' whilst the depot also benefits from its own fully-equipped

Top: Chris Bennett's growing fleet in 1982.
Above left: Chris Bennett unloading at Liverpool docks.
Below: A Familiar sight to the people of Cheshire, a Bennett's heavy haulage vehicle, 2005.

R F Feilding

Not for nothing are lorry drivers known as the knights of the road. It's probably because so many of them actually spend their nights on the road - making sure that food is delivered fresh to British supermarkets long before most of us have got out of bed in a morning.

Working round the clock is not something that many of us would want to do, but we thank those who have the stamina to do so.

Few people work such strange hours, perhaps only those who are brought up to a life where the working day normally begins before the sun rises can really take to the job. People like farmers for example. People like Reuben Fielding, whose local transport firm owes its eminence to his unremitting hard work burning the candle at both ends, an ethic learned from his farming background and his farmer father.

It is now some 50 years ago that the well known locally based transport firm of RF Fielding (Cheshire) Ltd had its tentative beginnings. Little did its founder ever imagine back then what a large undertaking his fledgling firm would one day become. Nor no doubt did he really antici-pate that from the age of 16 to over the age of 40 he would never have a day off, working every day of the week, with Sundays just like another day.

Above: Founder Reuben Fielding.
Below: Son of the founder Reuben F Fielding and a friend cycle alongside Dean Farm, where the family business began.

was beginning to give way to post war prosperity, but standards of living were still low, horses were still a familiar sight along cobbled streets, there were no motorways, steam trains still thundered through the countryside and few people had private cars.

As for lorries, there were plenty about, but they were small slow-moving creatures emitting clouds of diesel fumes behind them compared to the sleek and speeding juggernauts of today. The word juggernaut is incidentally, despite its Greek-looking ending, derived from Hindi and is an alternative name for the Hindu god Krishna whose statue was annually drawn through the streets of the town of Puri in eastern India on a huge chariot.

There may have bee no juggernauts on British roads in the 1950s but things were changing. And there were new openings for those with ambition and ability. One area was in road haulage. Large haulage firms had been nationalised after the war and major restrictions put on smaller privately owned firms. But the easing of those restrictions, cheaper fuel, the increasing availability of vehicles, and above all, improvements to roads and the removal of legal obstacles, would provide the springboard for many entrepreneurs to try their hand at the road haulage business.

It was in the 1950s that Reuben F Fielding left school to start work on the family farm - Dean Farm in King Street, in Woodford. Reuben's father, also called Reuben, had started the farm, and it still remains in the family, now run by the third generation of Fieldings, Reuben's son James Fielding.

Reuben Fielding was both born and bred in Woodford. When he began working on his father's farm, his father had one wagon which he used to transport farm produce which he both bought and sold.

The 1950s was an odd, half way, sort of decade. The 1940s had seen war and hardship on a worldwide scale. The 1960s would see unprecedented prosperity and a freedom unknown to previous generations. The 1950s however, were a half way house between the two. Post war austerity

Not that every new business had an easy start. Eventually Reuben junior bought a second wagon which he used for farm contracting, but then a driver smashed it up and the other driver left.

With one wagon and no drivers Reuben had to do everything himself; everything that is that was not done by his wife Gwyneth who helped from the first day in the office, taking orders off customers and taking care of the book keeping. Reuben renovated an old wagon and drove it doing deliveries after finishing his farm work.

Top left: Reuben F Fielding taking a well earned rest in the early 1960. **Above left:** Three generations of the Fielding family: founder Reuben (right) his son Reuben F (left) and grandson James (centre).

He then bought a second wagon from a scrap yard for £200, and did it up helped by Harry Thorpe who would subsequently assist in many such 'revitalisation' projects. Another one followed, it would however not be until 1970 that the first brand new wagon would be bought - a BMC which cost of £825. Little did Reuben imagine that in the opening years of the 21st century he would be paying 100 times more, up to £85,000 for a single vehicle.

Or perhaps Reuben in 1970 did envisage paying that much money one day. The 1970s were an appalling time economically with monetary inflation running at near to 30 per cent by the middle of the decade. Nor was that the only problem: difficulties in the Middle East had pushed up fuel costs to previously unheard of levels, whilst at home 'industrial action' a popular synonym for going on strike was crippling Britain's economy.

Many businesses optimistically begun in the post war boom of the 1950s now felt the cold wind of recession and closed. The better one's survived. Building up the business of buying and selling hay, straw and farm produce over the next 15 years led to Reuben becoming the largest farm produce merchants for hay and straw in the country.

This farming and contracting business is still based at the original farm in Woodford and is now run by Reuben and Gwyneth's son James. The couple also have a daughter Nicola who is a hairdresser.

But the hay and straw distribution business did not always run smoothly. In the early 1980s the Fieldings had a particular bad year; inexplicably, all went quiet.

Below: An aerial view of Dean Farm in the early 1980s?.

company's own distinctive green and red livery, though others are out to contract to other businesses. From just one person the firm now employs 280 staff.

RF Fielding now specialises in food distribution, delivering for all the major bakeries and supermarkets throughout Britain such as Tesco, Asda, Morrisons and Safeway. From having once specialised in distributing animal feeds the company now distributes anything sold in supermarkets: cakes, food, drinks and hardware. Goods are often taken into the warehouse and then broken down into smaller orders for delivery to regional distribution centres for onward delivery to local branches.

Within the large warehouse the operation is computerised 'order picking' working 24 hours a day seven days a week.

As a response to that downturn the business diversified and began distributing fertiliser. Working within a 150 mile radius of Stockport Reuben now sub-contracted for lots of haulage work to take out goods and then bring back fertiliser. This process led in turn to doing more haulage from existing customers. Suddenly the business began to grow. Though there was a warehouse in Woodford for general products this was soon nowhere near large enough. The need for more storage was becoming urgent.

Reuben had taken on Philip Howe as transport manager (he would subsequently become Managing Director) to help him with the increasing complexity of the operation. After 35 years at Dean Farm the need more space for the growing number of wagons, and the demand for extra warehousing, was acute. In 1991 RF Fielding moved the non-farm related part of the burgeoning transport business to Birdhall Lane, Cheadle Heath where the firm is still based today in a 240,000 sq ft warehouse.

With room at Birdhall Lane to expand the company could at last begin to spread its wings, investing in more vehicles, more staff and provide an ever better service to its clients.

And clients liked what they were being offered. More and more haulage work came RF Fielding's way, turning the tiny firm of fifty years earlier into a major name in the haulage industry.

From just one wagon in the 1950s the company now has 140 wagons, the majority of which are painted in the

Today Reuben and Gwyneth are still working in the haulage business and have warehouses in Sharston, Birmingham and Hamilton, Scotland. Their son-in-law Steve Spibey is Warehouse Manager, David Lowe is the General Manager, Paul McCarthy is Transport Manager, Peter Whitelegg in charge of the office and IT, Andrew Beswick is Company Accountant and John Kenyon is Night Manager whilst Phil Highcock runs the garage and keeps the wagons rolling.

As for time off, Reuben does now manage to take an occasional break. Today this knight of the road at last gets to spend some of his nights off the road.

Top left: *Reuben and friends holding a cup won for barrel rolling.* **Below:** *Reuben Fielding alongside one of the Fleet, 2004.*

FJ Goodwin & Sons

The first proper roads in Britain were those built by the Romans after they occupied England some 2,000 years ago. Though the Roman roads may have been very good, roads today have to take much more traffic: and happily our roads today are of much better construction.

Building roads, and even more importantly maintaining them, is a task which has grown and grown over the last hundred years or so as the motorcar has become king.

One of the best known firms in the field is a local company FJ Goodwin & Sons (Manchester) Ltd based at 50 London Road, Hazel Grove. The company address itself is of course a reminder that roads have been around for along time; London Road, the A6, having been built over the route of an ancient Roman road.

FJ Goodwin and Sons however isn't quite that old. First incorporated in the early 1960s today the company is a multi-disciplined civil engineering contractor specialising in foul and surface water drainage schemes, earthworks, site preparation, new road construction and road improvements, reinforced concrete substructures and landscaping.

But though the company may have only come into official existence in the 1960s the firm and its history goes back considerably further. Francis (Frank) James Goodwin, the company founder, was born during the first world war in Barrow in Furness. Frank's father was a seaman, his mother Josephine Duffy was from Clare Morris in County Mayo. She died when Francis

Top left: *Founder Frank Goodwin.*
Below: *Frank Goodwin cutting stone for St Peter's Cenotaph outside Manchester Central Library.*

was just three; tragically her father known as 'Duffy the Foreman' was killed in an accident in the shipyards at Barrow at around the same time.

Still in their youth Frank and his brother Joe moved from Barrow to Manchester. The brothers were very keen on boxing, and both boxed for the Holy Name team in Manchester. Frank met his wife Margaret Constance Connolly Carr through the boxing fraternity; she was from Cobh in County Cork and been to school in Dublin before moving to Manchester. Frank was a great friend of Margaret's brother Maurice who boxed under the name of Jackie Carr. Maurice was in the same stable, and sparring partner to Johnny King who was then World Champion, and boxed in exhibition bouts with him around the country.

Frank began his working life as a butcher, but he soon moved into the construction industry and became what was known in those days as a banker mason.

It was the early 1930s. Across Britain millions were out of work as a result of the great depression which had spread across the world after the Wall Street Crash of 1929. Yet though millions may have been on the dole many more millions still had jobs - albeit more often than not working for a pittance.

Frank was one of the lucky ones: yet he made a lot of his own luck, by being a first-rate worker. He served his time cutting and dressing stone for a Stockport company called Hopkins. He worked on piecework for Hopkins and soon gained a reputation for road building. Most of the roads in those days were built by hand using a stone-pitching method. He also worked for Fram and for George Wimpey during these dark years.

When the second world war broke out, because of Frank's reputation for road building, he was seconded to George Wimpey who had been given an open contract by the Government to build and repair RAF runways. Frank worked all over the country, wherever the demand took him.

If the building industry had been in the doldrums in the 1930s that situation had changed dramatically in 1939 with the outbreak of war. Civil engineers and builders were in more demand than ever before. Tens of thousands of defence-related construction projects were commissioned by the War Office to help defend Britain against the threat from Germany.

Above: *FJ Goodwin Staff pose for a photograph on Churchill Way in 1983.*

Frank and Margaret's first child, Michael Dwyer was born in the dark days of 1940. It was inevitably a difficult time for all three of them; when Frank was on a contract for any length of time however, he would rent digs and send for them both to stay with him, but he was mostly on the move. A second son, Francis James jnr, was born in 1943.

After the war Wimpeys offered Frank a job, but Frank wanted to start his own civil engineering business. He now employed some 30 to 40 men and worked in the private sector for companies such as Hopkins, Vessey, Fram and Wimpey constructing new roads.

A third and last son Sean Duffy was born in 1949. Sons Michael and Frank joined Frank in his firm in the 1950s; but despite the extra help from his two sons it wasn't all plain sailing running the business and they endured some lean spells with rates and profit margins very tight.

It was about that time when the firm was kerbing and flagging the A6 in Stockport that Frank was approached by the Council to carry out some contracts in the public sector. Frank and his staff's impressive work for the Stockport Council then attracted the

attention of the Hazel Grove and Bramhall Urban District Council, and in turn others such as Cheadle & Gatley UDC, all of which soon offered him work.

At that time the business was operating from premises in Barmouth Street in Bradford, Manchester. Frank moved the firm to Heaton Moor in Stockport in the early 1960s. He then rented a small yard at the back of Brewer & Turnbull removal company off John Street in Hazel Grove.

Frank also bought some cottages in John Street and converted them into offices. The cottages however, have long since been compulsorily purchased by Stockport Council and were demolished some years ago.

Most of the work in the old days was carried out by hand with very little machinery and it was a very demanding and stressful job. The company FJ Goodwin & Sons (Manchester) Ltd was formed in 1963. Unhappily its founder Frank Goodwin was to die of a massive heart attack on 13th March 1965, he was just 49.

Above: *FJ Goodwin's digger at work in Didsbury Road.*

Contracts of all sizes up to £2.5 million have been completed over the decades by the company, mainly in the Northwest region. Notable clients include AstraZeneca, British Gypsum, Stockport MBC, Cheshire County Council and many others both private and public.

That the company has expanded over the years and remains profitable is largely attributable to the degree to which it genuinely values its clients. Today it is heavily involved in 'Alliancing' - working as part of a team with other contractors and the customer from the outset of a project, at the design stage, and following it through to final completion.

Frank's eldest son, Michael, now aged 25, took the helm, ably supported by 22-year-old Frank junior. Youngest brother Sean turned 16 that summer and joined his brothers in the family firm immediately.

The three brothers continued to work successfully in both the public and private sectors, and in the 1960s were heavily involved in a variety of projects in and around Stockport.

During the following years the company expanded and bought a section of Brewer & Turnbull's site, and in turn Gosling's yard next door, and eventually a row of houses on London Road. The houses have since been converted into modern offices and together form the firm's current base of operations in Hazel Grove.

Recently a state of the art servicing facility has been completed where the company's fleet of modern equipment is maintained, having demolished an old servicing facility inherited from Brewer & Turnbull.

The company has kept going through many trying times, not least the three-day week of he 1970s and periodic economic recessions, which invariably hit the construction industry particularly hard.

Today the third generation of Goodwins are involved with Michael's sons Dominic, Patrick and Rory all now directors. Sean's daughter Rachel is also active in the business as its Environmental Training Manager.

Michael remains as Chairman, Sean is Managing Director whilst Frank has now retired.

The company is registered as Investors in People, and is Quality Assured to the ISO 9001:2000 Standard. It is also a Member of the Civil Engineering Contractors Association

When it comes to building roads, car parks, drainage systems, earthworks and enabling operations; reinforced concrete sub structures and slabs, bridges, retaining walls, landscaping and demolition - forget the Romans; FJ Goodwin & Sons Ltd is the name to remember!

Top left: Work under way on Churchill Way Mall, 1984.
Below: FJ Goodwin's Edgerton Road project in 1987.

Allied Bakeries - The stuff of life

Bread 'the staff of life'. Where would we be without bread to make sandwiches, mop up our gravy or to make our breakfast toast? Bread has been known for thousands of years, and baked by housewives since time immemorial. So important is the association of bread with domestic happiness and contentment that the term 'bread winner' still has a resonance long after its literal meaning has been lost.

For housewives making bread has always been a hard if worthwhile task. How many husbands coming home from the fields and forests ravenous with hunger salivated as they sniffed the air detecting the welcoming scent of newly baked bread awaiting their return?

No doubt thanks and appreciation were profuse, but that did not take the hard work out of the process. What housewives wanted was someone else to do the job for them. That demand led to the arrival of the professional baker.

For thousands of years now bakers have been working through the night baking bread so that it will be for sale fresh each morning.

In Britain small corner shop bakeries remained the dominating force in bread making until at least the second world war, but major changes in production capacity meant large commercial bakeries operating on an industrial scale would progressively challenge them.

That development was in part fuelled by the existence of new machinery and improved transport, such as the 20th century invention of the bread-slicing machine at Battle Creek Michigan in the USA, and the ever decreasing cost of motor transport making it economically viable to delver bread over ever wider areas from a single source.

Above: *An early Weston's Confectionery advertisement.*
Below: *Adding the finishing touches to iced cakes.*

Today Allied Bakeries Stockport handles more than 1.5 million products per week. Bread is baked fresh every day.

A modern bakery, producing traditional products, the Stockport Bakery employs 340 people across the site.

There are three automated plants at Allied Bakeries Stockport each of the Bread Plants produces every day favourites.

The innovative technology such as the plant automation using robotics on A Plant is groundbreaking. A new oven has been installed on B Plant at a cost of £1 million. The new Gold products on D Plant are quickly becoming firm favourites.

During 2004-2005 there was an extensive programme of improvements made involving the installation of a new ice plant, together with a liquid ingredient bulk supply system. Both new systems working in conjunction with the Scada data acquisition control system make.

Allied Bakeries Stockport one of the United Kingdoms largest and most modern bread production plants.

The Beacon and the Diamond satellite controlled ordering and picking systems have been installed revolutionising the dispatching of bread.

The spacious, modern bakery operated today by Allied Bakeries in Stockport developed from the small baker's shop opened in the early part of the 20th century in the Upper Brook Street, Manchester, by Richard Sharrock. Being an astute businessman as well as a Master Craftsman he soon owned two plant bakeries in that area, and by the 1920s these had amalgamated into a 'Tip Top' Bakery operating under the banner 'White Chief'. This was based in the Plymouth Grove area of Manchester and became a thriving concern.

In the 1950s the Sharrock family sold their interests to the Allied division of Associated British Foods. The company still retained the name of Richard Sharrock & Sons, the name lasting until the 1990s.

In 1952 the present bakery was built on a site which allowed for further expansion and development within the Allied Bakeries group.

Allied Bakeries was founded by Garfield Weston in 1935. At the time the company consisted of seven bakeries operating as independent family businesses. Today Allied Bakeries serves the whole of Great Britain and has the largest share of the British bread market, at around one third of the whole. The company also provides a wide range of morning goods, rolls, part bake bread for bake-off in retailers' stores and has a specialist bakery for the production of bread for sandwich makers.

The Weston family baking empire traces its roots back to the reign of Queen Victoria and to the one William Weston.

William Weston was born in London in humble circumstances before emigrating to Canada in the 19th century. In Toronto William's son George would transform the family's fortunes.

At the age of ten George started work as a baker's delivery boy: at the age of 17 he opened his own bakery. George then realised that big money could be made from selling fresh bread door to door. By the time he sold his business in 1911 George Weston had become a millionaire.

Above: A young Margaret Thatcher meets a bread salesman. Deliveries were made by horse and cart until the late 1960s.

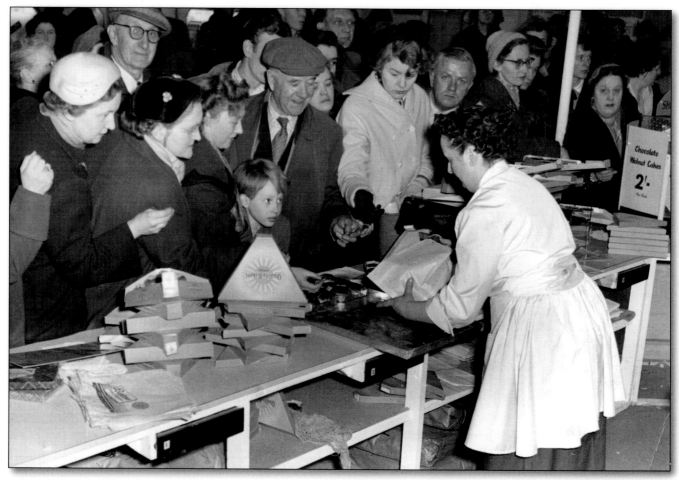

George Weston then made another fortune after starting a biscuit factory, and then a third fortune when he returned to the bakery business.

George's son William Garfield Weston was a slice from the same loaf. After having almost been driven out of business by the Wall Street Crash of 1929 he scraped together enough money to take his family back to its roots in England to begin all over again.

The first thing Garfield Weston did was to introduce British customers to Ryvita. By 1951 he had accumulated enough wealth to buy Fortnum & Mason's.

But in the late 1930s the Fortnum and Mason's purchase was still far in the future and Garfield Weston concentrated his efforts on building up a small chain of bakeries.

The late 1930s were not however the best time to get into the bakery business. The outbreak of war in 1939 soon disrupted supplies of flour, and the rationing of many basic foodstuffs soon told their own sorry tale.

Wheat for British bread came mostly from Canada and the USA. Hitler intended to starve the British into submission by sinking grain ships, and any other merchant shipping carrying supplies for Britain.

In the following years packs of U Boats haunted the sea-lanes of the Atlantic scouring the waves for unprotected shipping.

In Britain sliced bread became a memory. No white bread was produced after 1942. Similarly, attractive wrapping for loaves was put on hold and would not appear until the period of austerity came to a close several years after the war's end.

Happily the supply problem was eased if not solved. The introduction of the convoy system eventually turned the tide, resulting in far fewer vessels being lost to U Boat wolf packs. Britain and its bread-hungry citizens lived to fight their way to victory of the Nazi terror.

It was never necessary to introduce bread rationing in Britain during the war. Ironically, though many foodstuffs were rationed during the course of the conflict, it was only in 1946, a full year after the

Above: Crowds flock at a Bakery Exhibition in the 1950s.

German surrender, that bad harvests throughout the world made it necessary to put bread on the ration for the first time.

Today Allied Bakeries is one of a number of companies in the Associated British Foods Group (ABF). Other prestigious brands within ABF include British Sugar, Ryvita, and Twinings. ABF has interests throughout the world, stretching from Poland to Australia.

Allied Bakeries now has 16 bakeries and 12 depots producing high volumes of bread and rolls, both branded and own label, bakery snacks, sandwich bread and bake off products.

In addition to baking the Group distributes the products throughout the country. Each bakery has a dispatch and distribution operation, while there are a number of satellite distribution centres including Aberdeen, Edinburgh and Bristol. To give an idea of the quantities involved it delivers 15 million loaves, 10 million rolls and 7 million crumpets to 4 thousand outlets a week in 2 million baskets. Some 75 thousand orders are received a week.

Meet a great new TV star

Sunblest

Now! Sunblest back on TV... in a brand new wrap

Sunblest - the sign of good sales

Bread is the most basic of our foodstuffs; a prime commodity. No matter what ups and downs of the economy, no matter what changes in fashion occur, no matter what fads for fancy foods come and go, bread will remain with us forever, consumer demand persisting no matter how demand for other products may rise and fall.

When our far distant ancestors first ground wild grass seeds and formed the resultant flour into a paste to make the first bread they could not have imagined the consequences of their actions. From those primitive beginnings have come seas of Canadian prairie covered with swaying wheat, huge grain ships sailing across the oceans and enormous silos in docks across the world.

Step by step the history of bread making has led directly from that first stone-ground fire baked loaf to the modern baking industry and to Allied Bakeries in Stockport.

Above: A Sunblest advert from 1965.
Below: A Sunblest float with it's slogan 'The sign of good bread - fresh to the last slice'.

WM Nelstrop

In the 21st century, after nearly two hundred years in business, Stockport flour millers William Nelstrop & Co Ltd is still at the forefront of the industry, not least because of its latest state-of-the art 'PeriTec' process which ensures a consistent purer whiter flour, a product which meets the demands of the most demanding of independent bakers. The result is bread which has more volume, better colour and improved texture and taste: in short, the perfect loaf.

Lancashire Hill in Stockport has a long history of flour milling. It was on there that 19 year old William Nelstrop first set up a corn dealing business in 1820.

William Nelstrop moved into the steam-powered Albion Mills a year after they were built. He eventually became an important local figure, serving as Mayor of Stockport.

In 1893 the original Albion Mills were destroyed by fire; rebuilding provided the opportunity to replace all but one of the stone grinding mills with, what were then state of the art, 'Henry Simon' steel roller mills.

Top left: *William Nelstrop, founder.*
Below: *Albion Mills, 1895.*

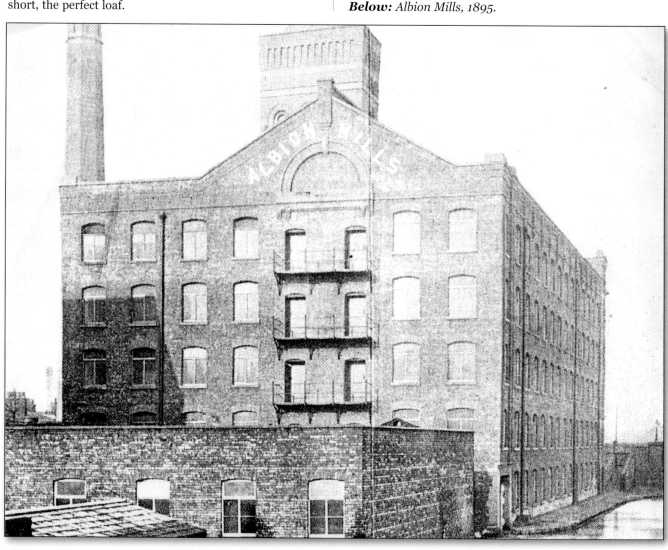

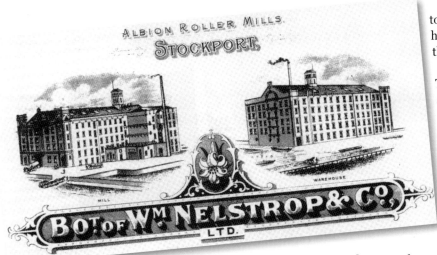

All the central Manchester flour mills were destroyed in air raids during the second world war. The remaining mills in the suburbs stepped up production to meet the shortfall. Nelstrops introduced three shift work schedules whilst staff stood by with sand buckets on the roof to douse incendiary bombs.

The mill escaped damage but then faced the difficult years of the 1950s ad 60s as mergers and amalgamations led to many small firms disappearing, taken over by national conglomerates. Before the war there had been 250 milling companies today that number is less than 25.

Using wheat from the UK, Canada, the USA and Europe, today Nelstrops produces 50 different types of flour and 120 different products such as special Pizza Lily Flour. Demand for other specialist 'ethnic' food products of all kinds is increasing too. Main customers are independent bakers, brand names and pre-packed own labels. At least seven different kinds of white bread flour are offered, three wholemeal flours, two brown flours, three malted flours, four soft flours as well as flours for such things as cakes and batter.

Co-operation with Satake UK, successor to Henry Simon, has led to the firm having the world's finest automated micro-chip controlled flour mills with continuous computerised on-line quality monitoring and full computer process control of wheat conditioning, cleaning and milling.

Satake's £3.2 million PeriTec system was installed by Nelstrops as a way to increase capacity within the existing mill buildings and provide the flexibility to increase its range of flours. The PeriTec milling system, developed by Satake of Japan, involves debranning wheat before milling. Debranning using both friction and abrasion can be varied according to the type of flour and bran required. The kernels are then passed through a hydrating unit designed to maximise water penetration and give a high level of control of moisture levels in the flour.

The slightest variations in the flour can significantly affect dough making so it is vital to maintain strict performance parameters by detecting variations and compensating for them. Wheat from East Anglia for example is very different from Manitoban wheat grown in Canada and enzyme characteristics, starch damage and protein have to be adjusted to ensure consistent fermentation.

There are three mills on site including a facility for stone grinding; one of the mills is dedicated to wholemeal, and all are remodelled every five years or so.

William Nelstrop's ran a small business with flexibility and a personal touch which is as evident today as it was then. Anyone wishing to speak to a director can do so: two members of the Nelstrop family are still part of the top management team in this the only independent family controlled flour mill in north west England, Scotland and Wales. All the directors have technical backgrounds and understand the importance of quality.

Continuing an unbroken line of family control the business is now run by the fifth generation of Nelstrops: Conrad Nelstrop is Chairman and was joint Managing Director with his cousin Paul Nelstrop until Paul's death early in 2000. Conrad Nelstrop's nephew Conrad Syers, the first of the sixth generation to be involved, is Technical Director whilst the Chairman's son, Matthew works in the sales department.

Top: A 1931 company letterhead.
Below: *William Nelstrop & Company Limited's management team.*

Stockport College - Learning from the past

These days we tend to forget the insatiable thirst for education that gripped the working classes in the late 19th century. Stockport's workers, young and old, were no exception to that national phenomenon. All kinds of new educational bodies were set up to meet the demand: Sunday Schools, Mechanics Institutes and Mutual Improvement Societies.

Today, more than a century after its foundation, Stockport College is one of the largest establishments of its kind. Some 14,000 students are currently enrolled on courses taught by an academic staff of over 600.

The College traces its origins to the Stockport Technical School built on the present site in 1889. Originally intended for evening classes, by the turn of the century the building also housed Stockport's

Municipal Secondary School, added to in 1910 by the opening of a new school for girls, the present Greek Street annexe.

During the First World War the annexe would be requisitioned to become temporarily the Greek Street Military Hospital.

In 1925 enrolments topped the 1,000 mark for the first time. Part-time day release courses had by then been introduced on a permanent basis, having been piloted on Saturday mornings since 1917.

In 1927 the school was renamed Stockport College of Further Education. Two decades of growth followed.

In the early 1930s electrical and typographical laboratories were opened. Engineering, philosophical and debating societies were formed alongside sports and recreational clubs.

But expansion brought its own problems: space was at a premium. The opening of the new Stockport School for boys at Mile End in 1938 relieved the situation. The following year new workshops totalling 10,000 sq ft were added to the technical school.

The second world war brought 3,500 RAF and Army service men passing through for specialist training, many being trained in the use of radar and radio.

By 1948 enrolments for day and evening classes topped 5,000 causing acute accommodation problems. These difficulties were eventually resolved by the conversion of a disused distillery in Hempshaw Lane into a College annexe for the building of textiles and electrical departments. The 1950s saw the demise of the textile classes, and the first full Ministry inspection since the war. The inspection highlighted the age and inadequacy of the College buildings and led to a plan to extend it.

By this time the student roll had risen to over 6,000, full-time staff to over 50 and part-time staff to over 200.

The further extension of the Hempshaw Lane annexe, following the secondary girls move to Goyt Bank, temporarily solved the latest space problem.

Then in 1960 the first phase of the College extensions was completed: a £307,000 block housing science, mechanical engineering, domestic studies and office accommodation. Phases two, three and four, providing additional laboratories, drawing offices, general classrooms, a library, refectory, lecture theatre and

multi-purpose hall, Students' Union and a Department of Building followed in 1964, 1970 and 1974: the latter replacing the old technical school.

In 1990 David Humphreys who had been principal for 19 years retired and was replaced by Dr Richard Evans.

The 1990s saw a decline in demand for training in engineering but an increase in the service industries. Travel and tourism, hairdressing, floristry and complementary therapies flourished.

At the end of the decade, the college sold its annex in Davenport and began to re-model the main site on Wellington Road South, creating bright new classrooms and facilities and installing state of the art equipment such as a new Computer Aided Design suite. In 1999, Peter Barkworth, nationally acclaimed British actor and twice BAFTA award winner accepted the college's offer to become patron of the college theatre and assisted in the development of a performing arts dimension to the college.

Since 2000, the college has become more involved internationally, in particular setting up links with China and the Gambia to enable students to study here. Links were also developed within Europe.

A new Principal, Peter Roberts, was appointed in 2002 and has led the college to achieve an even higher profile.

From January 2006 a merger with North Area College in Heaton Moor would give the College a new name: simply 'Stockport College' re-emphasising its role as a centre of excellence in tune with local needs.

*Left: An early 20th century view of the original site of Stockport College. **Top right:** The modern reception area of Stockport College, 2005.*

Stockport Market - To market to market

In 2005 Stockport Market was 745 years old. The right to hold a weekly Market was granted to the third Robert de Stokeport in 1260 by Prince Edward, Earl of Chester (subsequently King Edward 1). The Royal Charter permitted the Lord of the Manor (Robert de Stokeport) to hold both a weekly market and an annual fair within the walls of the Norman Castle on the present site of the Castle Yard.

The Market Place was the location of the last wife sale in England. It was also the site used for punishment: the stocks, whipping post, stretch neck and a dungeon. The Market Operator controlled a device called the 'brank' (a metal frame placed over the culprit's head, which had a tongue plate with sharp iron pins on the end which went into the mouth) designed to keep people quiet. The 'brank' can still be seen today in Stockport Museum's collection.

The castle was demolished in 1775. The Castle Yard became the site of a muslin tower where cloth was made. The tower was demolished in 1841 and the Yard was lowered in 1853 to make it level with the rest of the Market Place. A Cattle Market was then established in the area but when it later moved, the Castle Yard was incorporated into the main Market area.

By the mid-1850s Stockport Market was the most important cheese and agricultural market in the country.

The Yorkshire stone Farm Produce Hall (or Hen Market as it is fondly referred too), was built in 1851 and was used for the sale of fresh farm produce. Originally a single storey building, the upper part with its neo-classical columns and its balcony was added in 1875. Election speeches and

Royal proclamations were later made from this balcony, the last known announcement being made in 1910 when George V was proclaimed King. In 2001, this Grade II listed building underwent an extensive refurbishment.

This page: Early views of a bustling Stockport Market.

Market Days still bring the streets of Stockport to life every Tuesday, Friday and Saturday. There is also a bustling Flea Market every Tuesday, offering all kinds of weird and wonderful wares and larger than life colourful characters still working the 'gaff'. The Fruit & Veg. sellers can still be heard on rainy days shouting 'pick and pay without delay shop & shower'; and let's not forget the trader who regularly hangs coat-hangers on the back of shoppers coats as they walk past.

Stockport Market holds an annual Market Festival, which encourages the local community to join in its celebrations. There are also regular promotional events: an annual Dance Festival, Easter Promotions, Christmas Markets and occasional weddings at St. Mary's Church.

In 1861 Stockport Corporation ordered the erection of a Covered Market costing £4,423. It was constructed of timber, glass and iron along the lines of the famous Crystal Palace in London and was nicknamed the 'Glass Umbrella' as the sides were left open. The Covered Market Hall had nine bays when it was first built, but in 1912 one bay at the western end was removed to allow electric trams to turn the sharp corner by the Boars Head.

The 'glass umbrella' remained open to the elements until 1898 when Ephraim Marks (founder of Marks & Spencer) petitioned to enclose his stall - all the sides to the Hall were filled in soon afterwards.

The Victorian Market Hall almost did not survive: at the beginning of the 1980s the Corporation wanted to demolish it, along with other Market Place Buildings. Some 30,000 people signed a petition to save it. After an expenditure of £550,000 the Covered Market Hall reopened in 1985.

Over the years, Stockport Market has produced many colourful characters including quack doctors, fortune-tellers and organ grinders. There was the self-proclaimed 'man with magnificent muscles' who attracted customers with feats of strength in the hope that they would buy his corn cures. There was also an ingenious sweet-maker who enticed buyers to his stall by only employing beautiful girls.

With the recent refurbishment of the Produce Hall, the opening of a Tourist Information Centre and Museum in the old Staircase House, and the investment in the new marquee-style stalls, Stockport Market has never looked better. Soon the Covered Market Hall will be refurbished too.

Top: *The East End of the covered Market pictured in 1901.* *Below:* *Crowds of shoppers at Stockport Market, 2005.*

Frederic Robinson Ltd - Cheers!

On the last day of December 1935 the Unicorn Inn at 23 Lower Hillgate closed its doors for the last time. It was the end of a small piece of Stockport's history: the pub had been open since 1809. The closure of the Unicorn was not however the end of the Unicorn name.

In 1838 the Unicorn Inn had been bought by William Robinson. In the 21st century Stockport's Unicorn Brewery owned by Frederic Robinson Ltd and managed by the fifth and sixth generation of Robinson's is a continuing reminder of those early days in Lower Hillgate.

William Robinson died in 1875. He had lived long enough to see his son Frederic take on the Unicorn and begin its rise to become a major local brewer.

The year after his father's death Frederic began a process of lateral expansion: buying up pubs in order to have a guaranteed market for his fine ales. The first such pub was the Railway Inn, now the Royal Scot, at Marple Bridge. During the remainder of the decade and throughout the 1880s Frederic continued to buy public houses in Stockport and its surrounding area, pubs such as the Oddfellows Arms in Heaton Norris (rebuilt in 1978 as the Silver Jubilee), the Nicholson's Arms on Lancashire Hill and the Church Inn at Cheadle Hulme.

Before Frederic's death in 1890 the brewery had acquired an estate of twelve public houses. Leadership of the family firm now passed to Frederic's son, a second William Robinson. William Robinson continued the steady expansion of the brewery, opening a new ale and stout bottling stores in 1908 and adding to the Robinson estate, which by 1910 comprised over 30 houses. New offices were built in 1913 in Lower Hillgate, whilst the

Top: Son of the founder Frederic and wife Emma Robinson. Below: The Railway Inn, Marple Bridge, bought by Frederic in 1876 this was the first of Robinson's pubs.

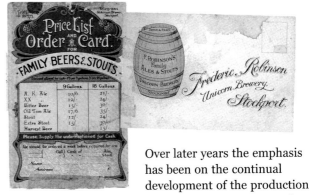

fleet of horse drays was augmented by the addition of three steam wagons.

Frederic Robinson became a limited company in 1920. In 1926 William, now sole Director appointed his three sons Frederic, John and Cecil to the Board.

When William died in 1933 his son John succeeded him as company Chairman.

Many fine pubs were acquired during the 1930s. But one at least was lost. Continuing expansion of the brewery sadly made it necessary to demolish the two hundred year old building where our story began.

During the second world war business continued as usual until 1943. On 27th November a fire broke out on the third floor of the brewery. It was midnight before the blaze was extinguished, yet incredibly the brewery was able to restart production within a week thanks to heroic efforts by firemen, three of whom were injured during the effort to save the brewery.

Robinson's acquired one of its two remaining local competitors Bell & Co Ltd in 1949: the sole remaining competitor, Richard Clarke & Co of the Reddish Brewery, would be acquired by Boddington's in 1963.

Dennis Robinson, John Robinson's son, joined the company in 1953 his brother Peter in 1957, followed later by third brother David. John Robinson was knighted the following year for his public service.

Sir John Robinson died in 1978 at his desk, shortly after the company had opened new facilities at the Unicorn Packaging Centre at Bredbury. Peter Robinson now took the helm.

In 1982 the firm acquired the Ulverston-based brewer Hartleys.

Over later years the emphasis has been on the continual development of the production facilities at the Unicorn Packaging Centre to support the extensive contract bottling and quality control operations which service the requirements of Robinson's many customers who supply supermarkets.

Robinson's draught beers can now be found in many areas of the country as guest beers supplied through wholesalers. These, together with the more recently introduced Smooth, means that Unicorn and Robinson's other brands are enjoyed in an increasing number of outlets.

The Robinson's estate continues to evolve, with selective purchases being made, and an increasing number of its houses offering food and accommodation.

Today there are five members of the sixth generation of the Robinson family actively involved in the company.

A new corporate image, intended to create a stronger identity for all the company's operations, the repackaging of its famous Old Tom strong ale, the legendary tipple first brewed in Stockport in 1899, and the export of its beers are all ensuring that Robinson's remains a name to watch.

Top left: Part of the Unicorn Brewery's motorised Leyland fleet circa 1920. Top right: Early price list and order card used by the brewery. Below: The next generation of Robinson (from left to right): Oliver, Paul, Neil, William and Veronica.

Co-op Bank - Banking on the future

The Co-operative Bank can trace its origins back to 1872, and has a rich history in Manchester and the surrounding areas. It began with formation of the Loan and Deposit Department of the Co-operative Wholesale Society. Four years later it changed its name to the CWS Bank and although in the early years it only took deposits and granted loans to the thousands of local retail co-operative societies, it was not long before it was acting as a bank for personal customers.

The Bank grew steadily with branches opening in Newcastle, London and Glasgow. After the First World War, the first in-store banking points were established in Co-op stores and more branches were opened in key locations.

The Bank unveiled its first branch in Stockport in 1964 at Abbey House, 57/57A St Petersgate, which it occupied until 1990. This was prior to moving to larger premises at 1 St Petersgate, which it still occupies today.

By 1972 the Bank, which was then known as the Co-operative Bank, had 32 branches throughout the country. In 1975 the Co-operative Bank became the first bank for some 40 years to join the Committee of London Clearing Banks and from then on it has grown at a rapid rate.

It further increased its presence in Stockport in 1996 when it took over the vacant Pyramid building as a service centre to its customers, which has been

instrumental in its growth. It also has a financial adviser arm, CBFA (Co-operative Bank Financial Advisers) that is based in the town's Regent House building.

Today, the Co-operative Bank is the only UK Clearing Bank to publish an ethical stance whereby it clearly tells its customers who it will and will not do business with. Since launching its ethical positioning in May 1992, thousands of concerned people who do not wish their money to be used for unethical reasons have had the opportunity to choose a bank which will not do business with unethical companies and organisations.

The Co-operative Bank was one of the first banks to offer its customers a 24 hour a day telephone banking service and it is now one of the biggest telephone banking operators in the UK. It has kept close to its North West roots, with service centres in Skelmersdale and Salford, as well as Stockport providing telephone banking to personal and business customers.

The Bank now has over 100 outlets and covering most major towns and cities in the country and is a member of the LINK consortium which means customers can use over 30,000 ATMs throughout the UK free of charge. In May 1994 the Bank launched the first fully automated Bankpoint Kiosk which is an unstaffed outlet that is also available 24 hours a day 365 days a year. Customers can use the LINK cash machine, an automatic deposit machine, and a video telephone link with the Bank's Armchair Banking Service.

Over the years the Bank has gained a reputation for introducing innovations which were later to be adopted

Left: A view towards the original premises of the Stockport Co-op Bank on St Petersgate.
Above: Stockport Pyramid, home of Stockport Co-op Bank, 2005.

by the rest of the industry. Since 1974 the Co-operative Bank has consistently offered free banking for personal customers who remain in credit and was the first Clearing Bank to offer an interest bearing cheque account called Cheque & Save.

In 1991 the Bank shook the credit card market when it introduced a guaranteed 'free for life' Gold Visa card. In 1993, the Bank launched another 'free for life' Visa card named the Robert Owen card after the social reformer who was considered to be the father of the consumer Co-operative Movement.

In 1996 the Bank introduced the lowest ever interest rate credit card - the Advantage card, especially designed for people who constantly borrow and so find a low interest rate more advantageous than an interest free period.

In 1997 the Bank celebrated its 125th anniversary by launching its Partnership approach, becoming the first company in the UK to produce a 'warts and all' social report involving all of the seven partners involved in the Bank's activities.

The Bank's reputation for innovation was again demonstrated in October 1999 when they launched smile the first full Internet bank in the UK, which was set up and runs from the famous Pyramid building. smile has been a breath of fresh air in the banking market, with its costs reflecting the reduced costs of Internet banking - offering its customers higher interest rates for savings and lower interest rates for borrowing.

The Bank made a return to the mortgage market in 2000 when it launched a green flexible mortgage.

The mortgage operation is also ran from the Stockport Pyramid.

In 2001, the Bank launched the UK's first ever fixed rate credit card, which offered a guaranteed rate of interest until 2006.

In 2002 The Co-operative Group board announced the formation of Co-operative Financial Services Ltd (CFS). The move follows the decision to bring The Co-operative Bank and Co-operative Insurance Society (CIS) closer together under 'common strategic leadership'.

In addition to over three million customer accounts, the Bank is banker to local authorities, many businesses and particularly the retail co-operative movement.

Balluff UK

The Balluff company was founded in 1921. Today it is one the world's leading sensor suppliers, providing innovative and practical sensor solutions for a wide range of applications and industries. The founder Gebhard Balluff started in business with a mechanical repair shop in Neuhausen, close to Stuttgart, South Germany for bicycles, motorcycles and sewing machines.

In 1956 the company developed patented electro-mechanical limit switches enabling Balluff to become an important supplier to the automotive and machine tool industries. Today the company is run by Rolf Hermle the grandson of the founder.

Production of inductive proximity sensors, now the company's core product, began in 1968 leading in 1971 to the first non-German subsidiary, Balluff Austria. The production of photoelectric sensors followed in 1978 with the introduction of microprocessor controlled limit switches shortly after.

Internationally known for the latest sensor technology and for one of the broadest product ranges of any sensor manufacturer, Balluff offers a complete line of sensors, limit switches, transducers and identity tag coding systems for monitoring parts through production systems. The sensor product line includes photoelectric, inductive, capacitive and magnetic as well as other more specialised sensor products to fit virtually any sensing application.

Sales offices are located around the world. Manufacturing takes place in Germany, Switzerland, Hungary, USA, Brazil, Japan, Korea and China.

The heart of Balluff's UK operation is at Finney Lane, Cheadle, Stockport. The business began life on 1st April 1979 trading under the name MultiSwitch. Its joint founders were Peter Ward, a former Sales Director for Hird Brown Ltd, a Bolton-based sensor company and Tom Coyne who until then had been Hird Brown's Sales Manager. With just one other member of staff, Pat Jacobs, the new business opened in Barlow Moor Road, Chorlton Cum Hardy in a suite of three offices and storeroom.

By the time the firm moved to the Old Mill in Finney Lane in Cheadle in 1982 the staff had grown to eight. Today the 'Automation Centre' in Cheadle provides work for almost 40 staff. Peter Ward's son, Martin, is still with the company employed as its Contracts Manager.

The aim of the fledgling firm back in 1979 was to market switches and sensors to British industry. These were supplied to MultiSwitch as finished goods by two overseas companies: Balluff their main partner supplying electromechanical switches and Jay Electronique of Grenoble, France from where photoelectric sensors were obtained.

With the development of the company and further exclusive agency agreements added to their profile, Multiswitch were able to service customers from the automotive, machine tool and factory automation sectors. These included all major vehicle manufacturers and their suppliers, from car seats to tyres.

MultiSwitch was sold to its principal supplier Balluff GmbH in 1997, which since the 1970s had opened subsidiaries in Asia, and the Americas, becoming a world name in the sensor industry.

The durability of Balluff's proximity sensors enables them to withstand harsh industrial environments and hence have earned for themselves the nickname 'fit and forget'. The uses of the sensors and switches is almost unlimited, applications range from prison doors to palace gates, bakeries to car factories and oil wells to the latest sources of renewable energy such as wind turbines and wave power.

The primary feature of Balluff's sensors is that they are non-contact with no moving parts to wear out. The benefit of this is that when fitted to machinery the product gives many years of trouble free service. This principle remains today, but advances in technology mean that sensors can now detect objects over much longer distances, work to much higher tolerances and even detect colours and patterns. Whilst the electro-mechanical switches, proven over so many years are still an important part of sales today, the technology is gradually being superseded by Balluff's latest state of the art electronic developments.

To celebrate the 25th year of Balluff in the UK, in 2004 all staff were taken to Balluff's major manufacturing plant in Hungary to mark the occasion.

For the future the general move of manufacturing industries towards the East promises great challenges for the coming years, however the development of innovative products directly meets the increasing technology demands of UK industry. With its new UK Managing Director John Radford, Balluff intends to continue to develop new products suitable for the packaging and printing industries, as well as supporting the UK's strong automotive industry. Future sales of sensors are likely to be increasingly hi-tech based on principles such as high precision laser and 'field bus' technology.

To provide a complete service for industry Balluff offer a full range of electrical connector systems facilitating the 'wiring' of its sensors. Almost every sensor is 'plug-in' rather than hard-wired therefore reducing wiring time and costs, but more importantly increasing reliability and productivity.

None of this would be possible in the UK without the highly trained and dedicated team at Cheadle, the majority of whom are from the local area. Indeed, they are a major factor in Balluff's continuing success from its beginnings in 1979 to the present day.

Left: *The original premises of the Balluff site.*
Below: *Balluff UK Limited's Cheadle premises 2005.*

Acknowledgments

Andrew Mitchell

Steve Ainsworth

All reasonable steps were taken by the publishers of this book to trace the copyright holders and obtain permission to use the photographs contained herein. However, due to the passage of time certain individuals were untraceable. Should any interested party subsequently come to light, the publishers can be contacted at the phone number printed at the front of this book and the appropriate arrangements will then be made.

True North Books Ltd - Book List

Memories of Accrington - 1 903204 05 4

Memories of Barnet - 1 903204 16 X

Memories of Barnsley - 1 900463 11 3

More Memories of Barnsley - 1 903 204 79 8

Golden Years of Barnsley -1 900463 87 3

Memories of Basingstoke - 1 903204 26 7

Memories of Bedford - 1 900463 83 0

More Memories of Bedford - 1 903204 33 X

Golden Years of Birmingham - 1 900463 04 0

Birmingham Memories - 1 903204 45 3

More Birmingham Memories - 1 903204 80 1

Memories of Blackburn - 1 900463 40 7

More Memories of Blackburn - 1 900463 96 2

Memories of Blackpool - 1 900463 21 0

Memories of Bolton - 1 900463 45 8

More Memories of Bolton - 1 900463 13 X

Bolton Memories - 1 903204 37 2

Memories of Bournemouth -1 900463 44 X

Memories of Bradford - 1 900463 00 8

More Memories of Bradford - 1 900463 16 4

More Memories of Bradford II - 1 900463 63 6

Bradford Memories - 1 903204 47 X

Bradford City Memories - 1 900463 57 1

Memories of Bristol - 1 900463 78 4

More Memories of Bristol - 1 903204 43 7

Memories of Bromley - 1 903204 21 6

Memories of Burnley - 1 900463 95 4

Golden Years of Burnley - 1 900463 67 9

Memories of Bury - 1 900463 90 3

More Memories of Bury - 1 903 204 78 X

Memories of Cambridge - 1 900463 88 1

Memories of Cardiff - 1 900463 14 8

More Memories of Cardiff - 1 903204 73 9

Memories of Carlisle - 1 900463 38 5

Memories of Chelmsford - 1 903204 29 1

Memories of Cheltenham - 1 903204 17 8

Memories of Chester - 1 900463 46 6

More Memories of Chester -1 903204 02 X

Chester Memories - 1 903204 83 6

Memories of Chesterfield -1 900463 61 X

More Memories of Chesterfield - 1 903204 28 3

Memories of Colchester - 1 900463 74 1

Nostalgic Coventry - 1 900463 58 X

Coventry Memories - 1 903204 38 0

Memories of Croydon - 1 900463 19 9

More Memories of Croydon - 1 903204 35 6

Golden Years of Darlington - 1 900463 72 5

Nostalgic Darlington - 1 900463 31 8

Darlington Memories - 1 903204 46 1

Memories of Derby - 1 900463 37 7

More Memories of Derby - 1 903204 20 8

Memories of Dewsbury & Batley - 1 900463 80 6

Memories of Doncaster - 1 900463 36 9

More Memories of Doncaster - 1 903204 75 5

Nostalgic Dudley - 1 900463 03 2

Golden Years of Dudley - 1 903204 60 7

Memories of Edinburgh - 1 900463 33 4

More memories of Edinburgh - 1903204 72 0

Memories of Enfield - 1 903204 14 3

Memories of Exeter - 1 900463 94 6

Memories of Glasgow - 1 900463 68 7

More Memories of Glasgow - 1 903204 44 5

Memories of Gloucester - 1 903204 04 6

Memories of Grimsby - 1 900463 97 0

More Memories of Grimsby - 1 903204 36 4

Memories of Guildford - 1 903204 22 4

Memories of Halifax - 1 900463 05 9

More Memories of Halifax - 1 900463 06 7

Golden Years of Halifax - 1 900463 62 8

Nostalgic Halifax - 1 903204 30 5

Memories of Harrogate - 1 903204 01 1

Memories of Hartlepool - 1 900463 42 3

Memories of High Wycombe - 1 900463 84 9

Memories of Huddersfield - 1 900463 15 6

More Memories of Huddersfield - 1 900463 26 1

Golden Years of Huddersfield - 1 900463 77 6

Nostalgic Huddersfield - 1 903204 19 4

Huddersfield Memories - 1903204 86 0

Huddersfield Town FC - 1 900463 51 2

Memories of Hull - 1 900463 86 5

More Memories of Hull - 1 903204 06 2

Hull Memories - 1 903204 70 4

True North Books Ltd - Book List

Memories of Keighley - 1 900463 01 6

Golden Years of Keighley - 1 900463 92 X

Memories of Kingston - 1 903204 24 0

Memories of Leeds - 1 900463 75 X

More Memories of Leeds - 1 900463 12 1

Golden Years of Leeds - 1 903204 07 0

Memories of Leicester - 1 900463 08 3

Leeds Memories - 1 903204 62 3

More Memories of Leicester - 1 903204 08 9

Memories of Leigh - 1 903204 27 5

Memories of Lincoln - 1 900463 43 1

Memories of Liverpool - 1 900463 07 5

More Memories of Liverpool - 1 903204 09 7

Liverpool Memories - 1 903204 53 4

Memories of Luton - 1 900463 93 8

Memories of Macclesfield - 1 900463 28 8

Memories of Manchester - 1 900463 27 X

More Memories of Manchester - 1 903204 03 8

Manchester Memories - 1 903204 54 2

Memories of Middlesbrough - 1 900463 56 3

More Memories of Middlesbrough - 1 903204 42 9

Memories of Newbury - 1 900463 79 2

Memories of Newcastle - 1 900463 81 4

More Memories of Newcastle - 1 903204 10 0

Newcastle Memories - 1.903204 71 2

Memories of Newport - 1 900463 59 8

Memories of Northampton - 1 900463 48 2

More Memories of Northampton - 1 903204 34 8

Memories of Norwich - 1 900463 73 3

Memories of Nottingham - 1 900463 91 1

More Memories of Nottingham - 1 903204 11 9

Nottingham Memories - 1 903204 63 1

Bygone Oldham - 1 900463 25 3

Memories of Oldham - 1 900463 76 8

More Memories of Oldham - 1 903204 84 4

Memories of Oxford - 1 900463 54 7

Memories of Peterborough - 1 900463 98 9

Golden Years of Poole - 1 900463 69 5

Memories of Portsmouth - 1 900463 39 3

More Memories of Portsmouth - 1 903204 51 8

Nostalgic Preston - 1 900463 50 4

More Memories of Preston - 1 900463 17 2

Preston Memories - 1 903204 41 0

Memories of Reading - 1 900463 49 0

Memories of Rochdale - 1 900463 60 1

More Memories of Reading - 1 903204 39 9

More Memories of Rochdale - 1 900463 22 9

Memories of Romford - 1 903204 40 2

Memories of Rothertham- 1903204 77 1

Memories of St Albans - 1 903204 23 2

Memories of St Helens - 1 900463 52 0

Memories of Sheffield - 1 900463 20 2

More Memories of Sheffield - 1 900463 32 6

Golden Years of Sheffield - 1 903204 13 5

Memories of Slough - 1 900 463 29 6

Golden Years of Solihull - 1 903204 55 0

Memories of Southampton - 1 900463 34 2

More Memories of Southampton - 1 903204 49 6

Memories of Stockport - 1 900463 55 5

More Memories of Stockport - 1 903204 18 6

Stockport Memories - 1 903204 87 9

Memories of Stockton - 1 900463 41 5

Memories of Stoke-on-Trent - 1 900463 47 4

More Memories of Stoke-on-Trent - 1 903204 12 7

Memories of Stourbridge - 1903204 31 3

Memories of Sunderland - 1 900463 71 7

More Memories of Sunderland - 1 903204 48 8

Memories of Swindon - 1 903204 00 3

Memories of Uxbridge - 1 900463 64 4

Memories of Wakefield - 1 900463 65 2

More Memories of Wakefield - 1 900463 89 X

Nostalgic Walsall - 1 900463 18 0

Golden Years of Walsall - 1 903204 56 9

More Memories of Warrington - 1 900463 02 4

Warrington Memories - 1 903204 85 2

Memories of Watford - 1 900463 24 5

Golden Years of West Bromwich - 1 900463 99 7

Memories of Wigan - 1 900463 85 7

Golden Years of Wigan - 1 900463 82 2

More Memories of Wigan - 1 903204 82 8

Nostalgic Wirral - 1 903204 15 1

Wirral Memories - 1 903204 74 7

Memories of Woking - 1 903204 32 1

Nostalgic Wolverhampton - 1 900463 53 9

Wolverhampton Memories - 1 903204 50 X

Memories of Worcester - 1 903204 25 9

Memories of Wrexham - 1 900463 23 7

Memories of York - 1 900463 66 0

Available in the Local Interest section of all major bookshops or direct from the publishers - telephone 01422 344344